openDemocracy Quarterly

The **openDemocracy Quarterly**
Series editors David Hayes and Tony Curzon Price

Series 1
Volume 1, January 2007. Europe and Islam.
Volume 2, April 2007. Turkey: writers, politics and free speech
Volume 3, August 2007. Europe: visions, realities, futures

The **openDemocracy Quarterly** is available by subscription. Please write to od-quarterly@opendemocracy.net for more information.

Europe: visions, realities, futures

Edited by David Hayes

openDemocracy Ltd.
London, England

© Copyright on articles by the following is retained by the author, published by **openDemocracy** Ltd: Ash Amin, Katinka Barysch, Simon Berlaymont, Krzysztof Bobinski, Michael Bruter, Ian Christie, Mats Engström, David Hayes, Judith Herrin, Philippe Herzog, Reinhard Hesse, Paul Hilder, Kirsty Hughes, Ivan Krastev, Petr Mach, Kalypso Nicolaïdis, John Palmer, Jeremy Rifkin, Pierre Rosanvallon, George Schöpflin, Ilija Trojanow, Theo Veenkamp, Frank Vibert, Aurore Wanlin.

All other articles are published by the author and **openDemocracy** under the Creative Commons Attribution, Non-Commercial, No Derivatives 2.5 License (creativecommons.org/licenses/by-nc-nd/2.5/).

This book was typeset by Mark Gamar (mgamar@free.fr) and Tony Curzon Price using LaTeX.

ISBN: 978-0-9556775-0-2

About openDemocracy

openDemocracy is the leading independent website on global current affairs—free to read, free to participate, free to the world... offering stimulating, critical analysis, promoting dialogue and debate on issues of global importance and linking citizens from around the world.

openDemocracy is committed to human rights and democracy. We aim to ensure that marginalised views and voices are heard. We believe facilitating argument and understanding across geographical boundaries is vital to preventing injustice.

Beyond and behind the headlines

We won't tell you what to think. We offer you a spectrum of ideas, from the people who have lived through the events, from those on the ground making a difference, from scholars with expert knowledge.

Our writers provide you with the background information you need to challenge the politics of any place. Every day, we publish new articles and opinions... sign up [1] for our regular emails or subscribe to our RSS feed [2] for constant updates.

A place to reflect—a place to be heard

Through our forums you can challenge our authors, question our visitors, express your views and read those of others. Help shape the world in conversation with other informed and opinionated citizens everywhere.

Become part of our global network. Come to our forums [3] and tell the **openDemocracy** network what you think.

Support **openDemocracy**—Free thinking for the world [4]

Everything on **openDemocracy** is free to read and free to share. It's not free to produce. Your support helps keep us independent and open to all—no matter where they live or what they earn.

Make a donation now [5].

URLS

[1] www.opendemocracy.net/registration6/joinMailList.jsp
[2] www.opendemocracy.net/about/aboutRSS.jsp
[3] www.opendemocracy.net/other_content/aggregation.jsp
[4] www.opendemocracy.net/donate.jsp
[5] www.opendemocracy.net/donate.jsp

Contents

Introduction, *David Hayes* 11

Visions 13
  How did Europe begin? 13
    The origins of 'Europe' 14
    The Arab advance 15
    Unifying the west 16
    Converting the east 17
    East and west against Islam 18
    A continent born out of political fragmentation and conflict . 19
  A letter for Europe 21
    Does "Europe" even exist? 23
    Europe is a politics, not a geography 24
    A constitution for Europe 25
    Enlarging Europe 26
  Three visions of politics: Europe in the millennial world 29
    Greens, anti-globalisers—which side are you on? 30
    Beyond 'Left' and 'Right' 32
    A fourth position: after the EU? 33
  Which Europe do you want? A map of visions 35
    Which Europe Do You Want? 35
    Superpower Europe 35
    Network Europe 36
    The Real EU 37
    Managing Globalisation 38
    Sustainable Europe 38
    Competitive Europe 39
    Social Europe 40
    Café Europe 40
    Safe Fortress Europe 41
    Europe of Nation-States 42
    European Democracy 42
    Constitution Europe 43
    Simple Europe 45
    Europe of Regions 46
    Federal Europe 46
    Europe's Law, Law's Europe 47

Executive Europe	47
Multi-speed Europe	48
Have We Missed A Vision?	49
An alarm-call for Europe	50
A Europe that stands still will be run over	51
For Europe, there is no future in disunity	53
America and Europe	57
Europe in perplexity	64
Three cycles of history	64
A confused landscape	67
Europe's green power	69
Europe's green path	70
A global alliance	71
The far side	74
European unity: reality and myth	76
The people on the stage	79
Realities	**81**
What the European Union is	81
What Europe is not	82
What Europe does	84
What Europe should be	87
France's 'non', Holland's 'nee', Europe's crisis	89
A communications failure	89
A democratic failure	90
Dutch sign on Europe's wall	94
The Dutch complex	95
A union of diversities	96
Five steps to Europe's future	97
Democracy in the European Union, more or less	101
Democracy's test	103
French fears, Danish dreams	104
Jean Monnet's ghost	105
Where next?	105
'Absorption capacity': the wrong European debate	108
A clearing wind	109
A new jargon	111
Adieu, Europe?	115
In a dark wood	116

CONTENTS

Waiting for the light	117
Bulgaria: the mafia's dance to Europe	120
The businessman	120
The mafia	121
The chief prosecutor	122
The police service	123
Turkey and the European Union: don't despair	125
EU talks: be constructive!	126
Cyprus: muddle through!	128
PR: highlight the positive!	129
Europe's new Ostpolitik: a Polish echo	132
The ghost of 13 December 1981	133
Europe's new *Ostpolitik*	135
Poland's politics of remembering	136
Tony Blair and Europe	139
A benign rupture	140
A litany of progress	141
A new road	143
An unwise promise	145
The balance-sheet	147
Futures	**150**
From ethnicity to empathy: a new idea of Europe	150
Ideas of the old Europe	151
Ideas for a new Europe	153
A politics of engagement	155
People to come	156
Europe and beyond: struggles for recognition	159
A community of others	160
A commonwealth for Europe	163
A third way	164
The European Union at fifty: a second life	167
The history of the present	168
A look in the mirror	169
The European Union in 2057	173
Grand themes vs everyday lives	173
Fifty years ahead	174
The challenge of uncertainty	176
European Union: from backdoor to front	178

- Ten myths about Europe 180
- European Union: after the reform treaty 185
  - The nation: from danger to redoubt 186
  - A treaty for tension 188
  - Democracy's pantomime-horse 189
  - A core Europe vs the rest? 191
- Europe at fifty: towards a new single act 193
  - Between maximum and minimum 194
  - A restored momentum 195
- Resources: links and further reading 198
  - Books 198
  - Institutes and think-tanks 199
  - Websites 199
- Authors of the articles 201

Introduction

David Hayes
11 August 2007

Europe is at once geographical expression, historical creation, cultural space, and political project. In the early 21st century, it is perhaps more than any of these a site of contention involving competing visions of its identity, boundaries and future.

openDemocracy, which began publication in May 2001, has tracked the arguments that have defined and divided Europe in this first decade of the millennium. In this collection of articles from our website, we present a selection of some of the outstanding reflections from the more than 200 extended contributions on this subject in our archive.

These years have presented major challenges to Europe both in the continent's internal evolution and in its relations to its neighbours and the rest of the world. Here are six areas where these challenges have been most acutely felt:

1. the project of enlargement of the European Union—which has seen the EU expand from fifteen to twenty-five members in May 2004, and then to twenty- seven in January 2007. This achievement is balanced by the unfinished business of southeast Europe, where a further tranche of aspirants awaits; but the biggest test of all is over the candidature of Turkey, the decision over which will be formative for the future of both sides

2. internal strains over the European Union's powers, institutional architecture, and constitution—especially following the referenda in France and Netherlands in 2005

3. the relationship with Russia—which has been marked by economic and political tensions as the chaos of the Boris Yeltsin years has given way to the country's economic recovery under Vladimir Putin; rising state confidence as a result of the oil-price boom and

energy-fuelled "resource nationalism"; disputes between Russia and her neighbours (Georgia, Estonia, Ukraine, even Belarus) as she attempts to recover control in a former sphere of influence, and resist the spread of the "colour revolutions"; and tensions over human rights

4. the need to respond to the post-9/11 threat of new forms of terrorism, in a situation where infringements of personal liberty in the interest of state security were a constant temptation; as the United States-led "war on terror" expanded, the question was increasingly posed of how far Europe could or should develop a more independent and integrated foreign policy in relation to the war, the middle east, Iran, aid and trade policy, and globalisation itself

5. sustainability and climate change—does Europe have a "green" vision for its future that is compatible with the political aspiration towards a more coherent union and the economic one of a bloc that can survive and prosper in a competitive global economy?

6. the issue of Europe's ethical foundation and cultural redefinition raised by the phenomenon of increasing diversity—as a result of immigration from the global south (Africa, Asia, even Latin America), assertion of religious identities in the public sphere, worries over long-term demographic decline, and divisions over core values

These are only some of the concerns that have made Europe a place of intellectual arguments where the questions and the answers matter. **openDemocracy** has been at the heart of the arguments, and this collection acts at once as guide, resource and stimulus to make sense of where Europe has been and where it is going.

Visions

How did Europe begin?

Judith Herrin

4 July 2001

> In the perspective of history, George W Bush's programme for Europe is flawed, Judith Herrin argues. Byzantine reality, not classical rhetoric, is the indispensable resource for modern understanding of the European Union's responsibilities to its citizens and neighbours.

George W Bush had a pretty mixed reception during his recent tour of Europe, but in one venue he was greeted with warm applause. This was in Warsaw, where he addressed a university audience stressing the common roots of Americans and Poles, with numerous references to John Paul II and Poland's heroic struggle during the second world war.

There are several notable features of this speech that seem to have been ignored. It appeared, for example, to regard the European Union and Nato as one and the same thing. It claimed that not only do 'we' share a civilisation and a culture, 'from Jerusalem and Athens to Warsaw to Washington', but, while constantly reassuring Moscow that America is a friend of Russia, 'we' must be particularly sensitive to the problems of the Ukraine, now trying to forge its own links with the west.

All European democracies, 'from the Baltic to the Black Sea', must have 'the same chance to join the institutions of Europe'. And later: 'The Europe we are building *must* include Ukraine', (my emphasis) while only being 'open to Russia'. This is quite simply an attempt to drive a wedge between the Ukraine and Russia, two Christian countries that share many historical features.

The speech was accompanied by a total silence about Nato's important ally, Turkey. This overwhelmingly Muslim society has also applied to join the queue for EU membership. In a speech redolent with soothing notions of United States-European Union cooperation, Bush praised the European opening to the east while also apparently trying to direct it to serve America's purposes.

I leave it to others to engage with the politics and strategy of the new administration in Washington. It is **as** a historian that I wish to respond. The gaps revealed by the president and his staff in understanding how Europe came into existence should be firmly restated, to correct their abysmal grasp of a history which has done much harm as well as good.

The origins of 'Europe'

The word *Europa* comes to us from the Greek, and we are all familiar with the Greek myth of how Europa was swept away by Zeus in the form of a bull. While Greece is the origin of many things, including that civilisation which Bush claims that 'we all share', it is not the starting-point for Europe.

Indeed, despite the profound influence of classical Greece and Rome on European government, on ideas of democracy and on the rhetoric of government from the Renaissance onwards, that 'rebirth' should not mislead us into thinking that Europeans today are their geographical inheritors. On the contrary, to understand the historical meaning of the term Europe, we need to recognise that its emergence came about with the final, shattering end of the Roman empire and its political legacy.

There can be no doubt that the empire of Rome suffered a long decline and fall brilliantly documented by Edward Gibbon and many who have followed him. The 'barbarian' tribes responsible for this collapse gradually replaced imperial structures by establishing their own kingdoms in the west. In the east Mediterranean, however, a new capital of the Roman world was established at what is today Istanbul, then Byzantium, renamed Constantinople in 324 ce (common era).

The city of Constantine was inaugurated in 330 as New Rome. It became the Queen City, the stupendous centre of the known world, which continued to identify itself as the Roman Empire. While the capital moved, the sea that was the true centre of the Empire remained the same: the Mediterranean. The Roman empire was a Mediterranean empire. Its granaries were in north Africa, Sicily and the Nile valley of Egypt. They fed the concentrations of population in both Romes. And Emperors were drawn from the African as much as the Italian or Adriatic coasts.

The move to Constantinople combined with the end of religious persecution as Constantine I granted toleration to all faiths. Christianity had spread rapidly from its birthplace in the near east, and again, the Christian empire remained a Mediterranean one. St Antony, the first of the Desert Fathers who inspired monasticism, lived in the depths of Egypt and spoke Coptic; St John Chrysostomos, 'golden-mouth', came from Antioch; St Augustine, the founder of Latin Christian theology, was from Carthage. This world was inspired by the holy places of the near east and its spiritual leaders lived in the great cities of antiquity: Alexandria, Antioch, Jerusalem, as well as the two Romes.

The Arab advance

In the early 7th century, a new force bent upon its conversion emerged in the east: the Arabs, inspired by Islam. From their base in Saudi Arabia they rapidly conquered the Holy Land, all of Egypt, North Africa, and under their leader Tarik, with the support of Bedouin tribesmen, would enter Spain in 711. By that time three of the five patriarchs had come under their sway—never to return to Christian rule.

The first and main objective of the Arabs was the Queen City itself, Constantinople. While the origins of Islam remain much disputed, it is clear that the Arabs had drawn upon a transformed version of the other two monotheistic religions—Christianity and Judaism—and worshipped the same true god. That is to say, the Arabs regarded themselves as the followers of the true prophet of that God and constituted themselves as a legitimate successor to the Christian Mediterranean empire. Their claim to this effect is written in their script around the Dome of the Rock on the Holy Mount of Jerusalem, a dome built by

Byzantine craftsman.

Had the Arabs captured the eastern capital, its population would have been similarly converted and their energies released to enhance the expansion of Islam. Only with the enormous resources of the great city, its unrivalled location, harbours and dockyards, its wealth, commerce and skills, would the forces of Arab Islam have been able to overwhelm Greece, the Balkans and Italy. The Roman Mediterranean empire might then have renewed itself once again, only this time under the green flag.

The Arabs were stopped at the great walls of Constantinople. Its strategic location, the use of Greek fire, the luck of the weather (a particularly hard winter which exposed the ill-clad Arabs to snow and forced them to eat their own dead camels) and above all the resources invested in a city of unparalleled strength and size, ensured the survival of the Byzantine capital. After a year's siege the Arabs were forced to retreat in 718.

The result was the preservation of a much reduced eastern Roman empire. Strong enough to last nearly a thousand years to 1453 as a medieval state, but never able to marshal the resources to re-conquer its former granaries or the seats of Christian patriarchy. It was too entrenched and determined to be overrun but unable ever to mount a return challenge for Mediterranean domination against a now wealthy and well organised Islamic polity.

At their most extended point in the west, the Arabs were unable to penetrate beyond the Pyrenees. Near Poitiers, Abd-al-Rahman al-Ghafiqi was defeated by Carolus *martellus* 'the hammer' (733). Similarly, the extreme northwestern tip of the Spanish peninsula was never subdued, and there the Christians of Asturias and Galicia clung to their own faith.

Unifying the west

This standoff shattered the unity of the Mediterranean world that had been forged by ancient Rome. A stalemate, whose central axis was the border between Byzantium and Islam, permitted a weak and parcellised northern world to survive. This, the northern residue of the great battle in the east, was united, in so far as it was united, by a single, highly organised religion, based on Latin Christian texts. This was the world that began to think of itself as Europe, a geographical entity distinct from the Mediterranean.

Europe, then, as we know, begins with the rise of Islam. Its founding moment was the Byzantine check on Islamic expansion into the peninsula of Europe from the east, the moment when the threefold division of the Mediterranean world began—in the 8th century. The division became a settled one between 800 and the end of the first millennium as Carolus, later called the great, Karl der Grosse, Charlemagne, unified the largest part of the European peninsula under his personal rule, allied with the pope, and established a permanent capital at Aachen, Aix-la-Chappelle. Not without justification did Alcuin, his skilful adviser who came from York, call him *Europae pater*.

Carolus was to divide his territories between his sons, who squandered his legacy in fratricidal competition. But the notion of a government of European dimensions survived both the northern raids and eventual settlement of the Vikings and Danes, as well as the southern raids of Saracen pirates established in Provence. And the papacy supported the Christianisation of all newcomers in the European area.

Converting the east

Meanwhile, in the east, Constantinople continued to develop as a major centre of culture and commerce, attracting scholars who made possible the almost peaceful conversion of the medieval Slavs and Russians to Christianity. Under the patronage of Photios, two brothers, Saints Cyril and Methodios, devised a new alphabet to represent the Slavonic spoken in the 9th century and translated the Christian scriptures, liturgies, sermons from the Greek original. Eventually Roman law, ancient histories, Greek novels and poems were also made available in Slavonic. Christianity became the dominant religion in southeastern Europe, visible in the numerous churches dotted over Romania, Bulgaria, Albania and the regions of Yugoslavia.

One hundred years later, under Basil II (976-1025), Prince Vladimir of Kiev was converted to Christianity and married the emperor's sister, who began to establish the first monasteries and churches in the Ukraine. Christians from Kiev who went north to Novgorod in turn met up with Scandinavian missionaries loyal to Rome and the papacy, who were converting the Baltic states and central Europe.

East and west against Islam

In this way, eastern Christendom contributed greatly to the conversion of Europe and the civilising of areas which had never been touched by the Greco-Roman traditions of the Mediterranean. Nor were the differences between what we now call orthodox and catholic so marked that the Christian forces of east and West could not combine against their common enemy, Islam. The faithful throughout Christendom mounted the first crusade and succeeded against all the odds in forcing the Fatimid governor, of Jerusalem, Iftikhar ad-Dawla, to surrender the city.

The crusading movement, however, also gave birth to the first documented pogroms against Jewish communities in the Rhineland and led in 1204 to the sack of Constantinople, a disaster even greater than the final fall of the city in 1453 in many respects. In a similar way when the Moors were driven from Spain, the Jews were also expelled. The narrow and intolerant determination of Europe may also be traced back to the western—but not the eastern—counter-assault upon the Arabs. For good or ill, awareness of the 'other' was always present and it regularly took the form of a hostility to the Muslims.

This is why President Bush's neglect of Turkey is striking. For his speech assumes that all those who should now join the EU share the same heritage—a Christian civilisation. But for Europe to grow and strengthen its own traditions, it must embrace the Muslims who have for centuries lived on its soil. Turkey thus represents a test case for EU expansion. As the conqueror of the eastern Roman empire, the

Ottoman inherited many elements of its civilisation, though it reformed them in a Muslim mould.

That this represents a profound challenge to the development of a fully democratic state that embraces human rights, especially with respect to the Kurds, and learns to live at peace with its neighbours, is clear. In its different way Ukraine is hardly immune from the same strictures. The point is rather that clear statements of principle and intention from our political leaders assist the processes, which must be the condition for full membership of a union such as Europe's.

The European Union that stretches from Scandinavia to Iberia is now poised to embrace the states of central Europe. A defining element of this welcome transition will be whether or not—on both sides—it will prove possible for Turkey to be engaged as well in the process of enlargement. I hope it will be. I look forward to a time when I can travel from London to Istanbul, and my friends and colleagues in Istanbul can come to London, without passports.

In order to assess whether this is possible, we need to look back at the history of Europe. What do we see?

A continent born out of political fragmentation and conflict

A continent that combines many traditions, with exceptional linguistic variety and cultural vitality, encouraged by the weakness of any centre with imperial pretension.

A continent whose best is its inner development and whose worst is its attempt at forcible expansion and the imposition of its values on others.

The attempt to transform this legacy, in a peaceful fashion, into a new and lasting arrangement should not underestimate how great a change this is, how difficult it will be and what deep forces will need to be confronted in achieving it. A profound respect for conflicting traditions and histories is called for. Not least with respect to the two great orthodox Christian countries of the east, Russia and Ukraine. Any superficial attempt to expand Europe's military and political commitments to the Crimea while remaining 'open' to Russia is playing with division, not overcoming it. Reversing the historical separation of east and west, Christian and Muslim Europe, is an admirable and serious ambition. This is no longer the time for divide and rule.

A letter for Europe

Reinhard Hesse

17 May 2001

> Too late for naïve hopes, too early for despair. A speechwriter to the German Chancellor Gerhard Schröder writes a sardonic, challenging letter to ask: where is Europe?

Dear **openDemocracy**,

I feel very honoured to be asked to open the *Europa* topic of your ambitious **openDemocracy** project.

I had a dream (or was it a nightmare?) that my literary agent urged me to write that one ultimate *non*-fiction book. You know, "the book only *you* can write," so that people will stand in line just to get a copy... and I said, taking what's left of my guts, "I could write a top non-fiction book on the most interesting question of our age: Europe!"

My agent paled. "Europe?" she uttered, struggling for her breath. "Don't you know that publishers run when they even hear the E-word?"

It's true. In the waking world, "Europe" is something which:

- the French know and enjoy, but don't want to bring to fruition;
- the Germans know and enjoy, but don't want to talk about;
- the British know and chose not to enjoy, because it seems to raise questions they don't want to answer.

And now that German leaders do talk about Europe?

As ever our French friends have proved reliable. No one could have seriously expected any French government to agree to making European agricultural politics national again. The Common Market is, to say the least, a very efficient tool to feed the beasts in "La France profonde."

So, when French officials welcome the debate only to reject the ideas, it only superficially comes close to the psychiatrist telling his schizoid patient that although what he's imagining is plain nonsense, "it's good we talked about it."

As a matter of fact, we do expect some counter propositions from Paris. Eventually we might even have a debate that takes us a step further than bargaining with Mr. Aznar over "cohesion funds" for the acceptance of "transition rules for new member countries." Or in plain language we will get past Madrid using its veto to profit from enlargement 3,000 miles away from Spain. But anyway, we love the European bazaar, even when it turns bizarre.

Things are not all that much better in Germany. Although we now have a proposition about European "constitutiveness"—carefully avoiding the big "C..." word that could cause so much calamity in the minds of cohesionists and splendid isolationists alike—the discussion hasn't really gone that deep.

Opposition parties bemoan a "theft of ideas." They are busy struggling with their own particular European past, such as corruption charges over the sale of an East German refinery to the French "Elf Acquitaine" group under Chancellor Kohl's government.

The general public has recovered from the surprise that Gerhard Schröder, of all people, should have come forward with a blueprint for Europe's future [1]. Now, we are all preparing to get back to sleep.

And Britain? Well, the honourable Sir Peter Tapsell, British MP—a member of the House, mind you, not a military policeman, even though his words might have suggested otherwise—has just reminded us what tunes to hum in our common Europe.

That particular gentleman urged the public to read German Chancellor Gerhard Schröder's suggestions for a European "constitutiveness" very carefully—that is to say more carefully than people had apparently read Hitler's "Mein Kampf." This time, our Tory politician continued, no one would be able to say he hadn't been aware of Germany's intentions to rule the world.

They do say that a few lunatics once in a while make democracy a worthwhile experience. Thanks, for the reminder that the "Achtung!-Schtrumpf!HeilHitler!" crap of B-movie fame has not altogether disappeared from the public debate.

On the other hand, the absence of any comment on Sir Tapsell's remarks by the Tory leader, Mr Hague, has been so obvious that it came close to trumpeting. This against the background of a courageous speech by the former Prime Minister, Mr Heath, and the tell-tale passive resistance by Prime Minister Tony Blair, who, instead of commenting, chose not to attend a meeting of European social democrats.

So would a book called "Europa" sell anywhere on the continent it is about? After so very many summit conferences we have come to a point where "Europe" is not, apparently, interested in any idea of itself.

Does "Europe" even exist?

A few months back, we were very happy to see "Europe" represented at the negotiation table in the Middle East. Javier Solana, doubtless Europe's most able diplomat, was trying to speak in Europe's name with Barak and Arafat at Sharm el-Sheikh. Did it matter? Yes, perhaps. But come the Israeli elections and the ongoing intifada—who cares about Europe?

Certainly, this conflict on the southeastern Mediterranean concerns us much more than an American in Nowhere/Michigan, or in Somewhere/Texas. But when it comes down to solving problems, it's not your European who is asked to help. Europeans pay: there is not a single Palestinian institution without European money, not to speak of Europe's well founded commitment to Israel.

Somehow, it's not "He who pays the band names the tune" any longer. It's "You guys pay for the band, and we name the tune"—even if we don't know how to sing.

So, once again, where's Europe?

Europe is a politics, not a geography

Europe's problem is not, as Henry Kissinger would have it, the lack of a single telephone number. Europe's problem is that there is no Europe. Politically, continents never match geographical lines; "Europe" does not have geological borders.

It is defined politically or not at all.

Even the idea of a "Europe" had to be brought to us from the outside, from the Muslim onslaught on continental territories. Since then have we made our minds up as to where Europe should be and extend to? The old Berlin wall? The Ural mountains? The distribution of "Le Monde Diplomatique?"

In recent days, we have begun discussing "Europe" in terms of the "European Union" [2]. And, indeed, the European integration as performed by the EEC, then EC, and now EU is a formidable success story for our continent. All the more so since this integration has been, literally, a common response to a bloody century and a half of massive, industrialised conflict. Europe made wars, and for once, Europe was able to make peace, at least with itself.

Call it pathetic, but Europe, or the European integration, is in fact the European peoples' answer to war. A common statement applying to bigger and smaller nations alike, expressing a Dutchman's aspirations for peace and prosperity, just the same as a Greek woman's. And, after we have overcome that unnatural cold war division, it is only too natural that Poles, Hungarians, Czechs and the Baltic peoples should share these hopes.

But do the Europeans still remember what they have promised themselves?

This Europe has been able to re-integrate Germany into the family of peoples—despite all the crimes that were committed in Germany's name, by German people and soldiers.

This same Europe has been able to make an enormous effort of reconciliation. To treat as reconcilable conflicts of interests what were once irreconcilable clashes of sovereignty between sworn enemies. Our peoples conceive themselves as Europeans without asking; they cross borders without showing their passports—unless they enter Britain, that is—and since the fall of the "Iron Curtain," they have a down-to-earth idea of what Europe could be, from Dublin to Dubrovnik.

But something is not happening.

We are Europeans on the ground. We are Europeans in our stomachs, as a succession of food crises has shown, but we are not Europeans in our heads.

There was the "Nice" conference [3]. It wasn't a failure. Bearing in mind all the conflicting interests, governments came to a fair conclusion that would allow the so-called "candidate states" to join once they had carried out their economic reform program.

But will enlargement make a better Europe? Some disturbing figures spring into my mind. Although German-French relations remain good, only 14 per cent of German schoolchildren learn any French. And less than 10 per cent of French students venture into German. Let's not ask about how things are in this respect in Britain...

We do have a certain "cultural penetration." Kids in London might know about "Einstürzende Neubauten," long gone over here. German adolescents will be aware of the "Trainspotting" image and way of life. "Intimacy," filmed in London, based on Hanif Kureish's stories, by a French director who is renowned in Germany, was awarded the "Golden Bear" of the Berlin film festival.

In politics, nothing, so far, corresponds even to this. Given the, at best, technocratic results of the Nice conference, political hopes are now focussed on the "Post-Nice-process"—another conference, in 2004, and between now and then a "Constitutional Debate."

A constitution for Europe

Now, a "Constitutional Debate" is about as funny as a baby's funeral. Unless perhaps, it strives for new principles, which express and respond to feelings of powerlessness, which is what new constitutions ought to do. Instead, our governments intend to discuss the division of competences between "Bruxelles," the National states and the respective regional governments.

This needs to be done. But will it enhance people's enthusiasm?

It is true that European policymakers still need to explain the limits and advantages of truly European decision making to the likes of you and me. "Subsidiarity" may be a ugly word but it describes pretty well what we are all after: A common will on the highest level, best practices for everyone on the lowest level he or she is concerned with. In other words: let a "strong" European government make our voice heard in the world—and let's make an effort to achieve that—and let a democratic, free Europe come up from its roots.

A European "constitution" brought about from above by the governments of our national states would not, I'm afraid, help a lot. At least it would not be enough to convince European women and men to seize the grand opportunity we have within our reach to build a common continent, free and democratic, modern and creative, with strong institutions of justice and, yes, a place where people feel "at home" in their homes.

Instead, a vague sentiment of alienation takes over, and a lot of concern: concern of those in the smaller states worried not to be taken over by the "big three," concern of those living in border areas over the influx of cheaper workforce from tomorrow's new member states, concern over how to safeguard internal and external security.

Enlarging Europe

The greatest challenge for our generation is not so much to build the European "superpower" Tony Blair envisioned in his Warsaw speech, but to make sure that the process of European enlargement leads to a good and prosperous end.

To my knowledge, French people are much more enthusiastic about enlargement to the east than the French political class. The opposite holds for Germany, where politicians want the opening, and people are rather afraid. And Britain? Britain has not even joined the "Euro" zone. Do you hear me there at all?

There is too much rationality about European enlargement and an obvious and dangerous lack of popular concern with it. Fears, yes, but commitment, no.

Maybe, we ought to listen a bit more closely to the sounds from the chamber orchestras of the "smaller units"—possibly, but not necessarily equalling the smaller states. Maybe we ought to remember that "Europe" is also a common space and a history of values other than slaughtering sheep and cattle for the sake of regulating market prices.

Once again, recall that "Europe" is not a geographical imperative. "Europa" is something designed by the will of peoples who feel and know a certain common interest. An idea of European life.

Do we have this idea? Can we charm Non-EU-European people with it? And, if the peoples want it, will we speak of it with one voice—without losing our mother tongues?

The other day, a German friend teaching in Washington D.C. passed by. He was curious to find out about the "Europa" debate and anxious, like most German intellectuals, that perhaps it ought not to be Germany to push ahead for "final status" discussions. He wasn't then aware of Sir Tapsell's narrative, but fears of that sort prevail.

And then, this friend added a striking remark. "You know" he said, "the only place where I feel genuinely European is the U.S. Over here, you can be German, English or Italian. But over there, you quickly find out that you represent a different, a truly European culture and tradition."

Maybe we should all propel ourselves across the Atlantic and learn a little "recount" about our home continent from over there.

So I can't answer the question you have posed—how to become European, and what it will mean when it happens. But the last few years have taught me that it is necessary to try and find an answer, and that it won't come from an intergovernmental meeting.

Yours truly,

Reinhard Hesse

URLS

[1] www.spd.de/english
[2] europa.eu.int/
[3] europa.eu.int/comm/archives/igc2000/index.htm

Three visions of politics: Europe in the millennial world

Ian Christie

30 May 2002

> The range of global political possibility has been transformed by post-Cold War turbo-capitalism. A new mapping of the political faultlines defines 'high stakes', 'shared values', and 'natural orders' as competing versions of the European future. But could there yet be a fourth, involving the demise of the EU itself?

When working at the Henley Centre [1] for Forecasting in the mid-1990s I developed a set of three scenarios based on an analysis of changing values and political faultlines. All three scenarios (or better, summaries of political outlooks and cultures) amounted to clusters of attitudes and political positions that would be powerful features of the millennial world in the West.

The scenarios were these:

A 'high stakes' model of development (US-dominated, depending on liberalised markets, economic growth, aggressive development of science and technology, and diffusion of American products, services and commercial values).

A 'shared values' model (broadly social democratic—under pressure from the 'high stakes' approach to global market development; a model of politics and economic development emphasising social capital, tolerance, multiculturalism, consensus and limits to social and economic inequalities).

What we called 'natural orders'—covering Greens, fundamentalists, localists and communitarians of left and right, and also neo-fascists. 'Natural orders' covers the protesters against the latest wave of the Enlightenment and Industrialism i.e. globalisation and EU integration.

The third, 'natural orders' cluster spans both left and right in the traditional classification of political alignments: it contains protests by *local and national* interests against the homogenising, top-down capitalist forces that are shaping the values, tempo, environments and organisation of modern societies. What links all of them is the non-Enlightenment view that there are *natural limits or imperatives* that science, progress and secular rational humanism cannot ignore. Some see these as purely environmental; some—on what we have always called the Right—see them as social and cultural, or even racial as well.

Greens, anti-globalisers—which side are you on?

The demise of socialism and communism has made the world open up to the latest wave of top-down universalising industrialism from the West. And it has revealed anew the older faultlines in the Enlightenment—tensions that run through whole societies, cultures, political parties and also individuals.

These are the tensions between the light and dark sides of universalism, embodied in a number of key oppositions:

Between the ideal of global human rights and democracy, and the flattening of local communities by more homogenised national and cosmopolitan cultures; between the benefits of scientific and technical progress (longevity, better health, better mobility) and the cultural, social and environmental drawbacks; between the tempo of commercialised, competitive life and that of more sociable communities; between the disrespect of modernity for tradition, and the deep attachment to older forms of community and identity; between the benefits of secularisation (tolerance, rational governance) and the drawbacks of the fading of religious culture in the West (triviality, rootlessness, the risk of nihilism and personal meaninglessness).

Most of us are uneasy hybrids of rationalist and romantic—a tension resolved so far in the West through the unheroic medium of consumerism, but one that is always liable to disrupt personal or social equilibrium.

These tensions have always cut across simple Left and Right divisions ever since the Enlightenment and the rise of Romanticism, but they were obscured in large part by the Cold War. The rise of environmentalism has revealed these tensions in a new light, as has the wave of globalisation since the mid-1980s.

Environmentalism is split between green modernisers, who hold to varieties of pro-Enlightenment positions, and 'deeper' Greens whose localism, spirituality and anti-capitalist stance can locate them simultaneously in places associated with the far left or right. Similarly, anti-globalisers occupy a spectrum from those concerned to humanise capitalist globalisation, to those resisting it in the name of localism, self-governance, religion or varieties of socialism.

The world we are in is one where a struggle is occurring within the Enlightenment-Industrial tradition, between the present American 'high stakes' culture and the broadly (but not exclusively) European 'shared values' perspective—what I have also called the struggle between a 'frontier' view of progress that now dominates the USA and global capital, and a 'chastened' view of the Enlightenment 'project' that is most credible in the EU and among a minority of corporations. This struggle is complicated by the intellectual and political guerrilla warfare being conducted on its fringes, and sometimes in its heartland, by 'natural orders' cultures—from Deep Greens to Le Pen, from al-Qaida to Adbusters.

For the struggle for 'natural orders' cultures is not just against their obvious adversaries in the cosmopolitan world system, but against *each other's* attempt to claim this perspective for themselves. Thus, George Monbiot [2] is horrified that he is being cited by the far right, but his 'natural orders' perspective on globalisation is far from the only one, and in many ways the straightforward 'blood and soil' line peddled by the hard right in France looks like a more coherent position than Monbiot's.

Monbiot's sought-for position is in many ways a very desirable one— but like democratic Socialism it takes a lot of explaining. There is no doubt that some ecological themes could yet be taken up by far right groups, just as Pim Fortuyn's movement has managed to appropriate some liberal ones and connect them to an anti-Muslim, anti-immigrant message. The force might yet be with the simplifiers in the Natural Orders world—fundamentalists and local reactionaries—and we may yet see more conflict between varieties of Green radicals and the 'far right' movements. The killing of Pim Fortuyn by a radical animal rights protester is—one hopes—an isolated incident. But it can be seen as a grisly illustration of what could happen if the 'left' elements in the Natural Orders cultures on the margins of modern politics see the banner of opposition to a corrupt, short-sighted and complacent political establishment being seized by the reactionary and racist ones.

Beyond 'Left' and 'Right'

One perspective on this whole complex of issues is to argue that the major faultline in twenty-first century politics is the one emerging between *cosmopolitans* and *communalists/localisers*, and that for right and left alike this is a baffling and deeply disquieting situation.

The pro-Enlightenment cosmopolitans are divided between neo-liberals and social democrats/environmentalists, and the 'natural orders' spectrum is divided between neo-fascists, religious fundamentalists, communitarian democrats such as John Gray, and varieties of radical environmentalists.

Thus, adopting a pro-Enlightenment cosmopolitan position can bring one into alliance with people one doesn't want to support (e.g. free trade neo-liberals and GM food barons); and being a Green anti-globaliser now seems to involve having common ground with the likes of Le Pen.

These tensions, always present in modern politics, are coming out in force now that the big Left-Right confrontation has faded away. Arguing for a locally sensitive, pluralist and environmentally sound cosmopolitanism (a 'shared values' scenario) can be extremely hard to do in straightforward terms when up against the 'natural orders' arguments of the localist right—who are now finding new 'modernised' ways to get their message over to the proponents of the 'high stakes' and 'shared values' cultures.

And as Anthony Barnett has argued, this is not just a problem for social democrats: the pro-market corporate right (favouring the 'high stakes' scenario) is in some ways more threatened by the localist/nativist 'natural orders' hard right than it is by the left.

It is now widely accepted that some serious attempt must be made to make globalisation more humane, environmentally responsible and less threatening to local community and identity. But to achieve this aim could be described as the greatest challenge of the era.

There is no escaping the fact that political universalism and economic progress have combined to produce not only many benefits but also a less diverse set of societies and cultures, and that the homogenising process seems set to continue. How does the recognition and reassurance of the best in local identities fit with the cosmopolitan projects of the EU and the 'international community'?

The failure of the globalising elites to address this issue is now plain for all to see. The European Commission, the G8, the WTO and NAFTA have all given ample ammunition to the worst as well as the best of the 'natural orders' cultures, which now have to be taken with the utmost seriousness. One might add that we need powerful arguments to be rehearsed in academe for 'chastened universalism' and for ways to reconcile Enlightenment values with desirable local diversity—a task neglected while many supposedly progressive thinkers have indulged in 'postmodernist' Enlightenment-bashing and celebrations of cultural relativism.

But that said, is there really any scope for 'natural orders' scenarios to dominate our future? Surely their role in modern societies is simply to challenge and harass the leading cultures—the American 'high stakes' model and the kinder, gentler 'shared values' model—whose hegemony is assured? Surely the governments of the future will be dominated by varieties of these political cultures?

A fourth position: after the EU?

The answer to these questions is a probable, but not certain, yes. Only probable, because the upsurge of anti-globalisation sentiments in so many forms should give pause for thought.

Consider this. One scenario for 2020 that no-one has been taking seriously is the disintegration of the EU as we know it, and the emergence of a right-nationalist alliance of states. Yet this looks like a possible outcome of the following confluence of events:

- more Islamist terror in the West (very likely).

- more pressure for illegal immigration from a more turbulent Middle East/Maghreb (very likely).

- more communal conflict in EU cities with large Islamic/black populations (likely).

- at least one big economic recession (possible) and severe pressure on the Euro (possible).

- and major problems of unemployment and inappropriate interest rates across EU regions (likely).

- strengthening of far right and knock-on influence on mainstream right politics (possible).

As the sociologist Peter Berger [2] has said, the modernisation process—which never finishes—exacts a high price in terms of human meaning. It is immensely disruptive of settled identities and communal bonds, and of the relationship between past and future.

The millennial commercial globalisation we are living through is the latest wave of modernisation, and perhaps the most disruptive yet. Rather than being surprised by the upsurge of varieties of 'natural orders' resistance, we should wonder that it took so long for them to hit out after the end of the Cold War and the worldwide offensive of triumphalist frontier capitalism.

URLS

[1] www.henleycentre.com/henley_views.phtml
[2] www.guardian.co.uk/Columnists/Column/0,5673,707532,00.html

Which Europe do you want? A map of visions

Paul Hilder

19 March 2003

> If you don't know where to start in the European labyrinth, this might be a good place. What is Europe for? Which Europe do we want? As the European Constitution is drafted, a bewildering variety of visions for the continent have been put forward. Here we, and our contributors, map the terrain.

Which Europe Do You Want?

Get involved on the Future of Europe discussion [1] board, or email your thoughts to openEuropa@openDemocracy.net

Superpower Europe

This is the idea of Europe becoming a new superpower in the world, or a counterweight to the US. It involves the EU taking on new responsibilities for foreign and defence policies.

Michel Barnier [2], European Commissioner: "Europe is a point of balance... between different regions of the world. We cannot leave all these big countries and continents such as Russia, China, India and Africa in a bilateral tête-à-tête with the US—we need a pluralist, multipolar dialogue... I do not reproach the US for their power or their force: I do reproach the Europeans for their weakness.

"I am not a partisan of the idea that Europe has to choose its policy and destiny in relation to the US. It must do it according to its own identity, its own interests and its place on the geographical map... Because of our history and our geography, it seems to me we can facilitate the chances of peace and stability in the world. But to do that, we have to have a willingness to play this role and be organised for it...

"If the US sometimes see themselves as the only superpower, it is for the EU to demonstrate that it is not exactly like that, and that there is another power in the world—an economic, commercial, monetary, political power—that expects to play its part... We cannot become a political power without a real common defence and without a coherent external policy." Read more [2]

Want to argue for or against Superpower Europe?
Email openEuropa@openDemocracy.net
or post on the discussion board [1]

Network Europe

Network Europe is partly a description of how Europe works at the moment and partly a vision of how it should develop. It is a complex, multifaceted idea of a unique political construction, difficult for some to engage with.

Manuel Castells [3], theorist: "The European Union is essentially organized as a network that involves the pooling and sharing of sovereignty, rather than the transfer of sovereignty to a higher level. Together, its institutions epitomize the network state...

"The EU does not supplant the existing nation-states. On the contrary, it is a fundamental instrument for their survival... a complex and changing geometry of European institutions that combines the control of decision-making by national governments (the European Council, its rotating presidency, and regular meetings of the Council of Ministers); the management of common European business by a euro-technocracy, directed by the politically appointed European Commission; and the symbolic expressions of legitimacy in the European Parliament, the Court of Justice and the Court of Auditors.

"The relentless negotiations within this set of institutions, and between the national actors pursuing their strategies, may look cumbersome and inefficient. Yet it is precisely this indeterminacy and this complexity that make it possible to accommodate in the EU various interests and changing policies..." Read more [3]

Want to argue for or against Network Europe?
Email openEuropa@openDemocracy.net
or post on the discussion board [1]

The Real EU

This is an idea of pragmatic and incremental development, which takes pieces from many other visions (federalism, Network Europe, Law's Europe) and stitches them together into a structure which might have practical benefit but be acceptable to the many different member states and political positions. It has many incarnations. "The real EU" is typically the second-favourite guiding ideal of European players. (Most prefer one of the others.)

Ricardo Perissich [4], Telecom Italia: "To build the Real Europe, we still need a clearer definition of the borderlines between what is European and what is national, for their leaner and more effective management. European legislation, for example, is well renowned for being both barely comprehensible and excessively bound up in red tape...

"The solution is very simple: replace the directives with directly applicable regulations. Of course, this requires acceptance by national parliaments of a strong measure of centralisation. It therefore presupposes a clearer definition of roles. Approached in these terms, 'European Economic Government' is no more than the organisation into a coherent programme of the many and varied tools which the Union already has at its disposal... Europe will probably have to resign itself to long-term cohabitation with an institutional system based on the co-existence of strong supra-national vs. inter-governmental elements." Read more [4]

Want to argue for or against the Real EU?
Email openEuropa@openDemocracy.net
or post on the discussion board [1]

Managing Globalisation

According to this vision, the European Union needs to be, not an uncritical advocate of uncontrolled globalisation, but a democratic manager of supranational forces for the good of all.

Erkki Tuomioja [5], Finnish foreign minister: "We live in a world where global market forces (even more threatening because of their anonymity) undermine or dilute the instruments we have historically employed to steer our economies and redistribute wealth. Globalisation thus poses a demand to develop strong new democratic policies and institutions for international and global governance.

"It would be nice to be able to say that we have already established the institutions for this. Unfortunately, many people see organisations such as the European Union and the World Trade Organisation as being the problem, rather than the solution...

"Voters... are surely right to insist, quietly but in huge numbers, that the EU must address the evident powers and importance of global change, from international corporations to the regulation of trade, finance and communications. This, after all, is in large part what it is about. By all means let us have a discussion on the nature of the European constitution... But it will be a hollow debate unless it tells us how this constitution will help Europeans confront globalisation and make corporations, NGOs, and other international bodies more accountable." Read more [5]

Want to argue for or against Managing Globalisation?
Email openEuropa@openDemocracy.net
or post on the discussion board [1]

Sustainable Europe

This vision proposes that sustainability and the "green agenda," both at home and in the world, should be the new mission, replacing the vision of a continent at peace that inspired Europe after the Second World War.

Ian Christie & Rebecca Willis [6], analysts: "The Union needs a vision that is about ends and not only means—an idea of the European good life and the kind of world in which European well-being and that of others can be sustained. It should start with the one policy area that really does command consensus and inspire European citizens—the environment.

"A politics of quality of life has the potential to re-connect the policy-making elite to Europe's citizens, by moving away from the technocratic ethos which gave us the disenchantment surrounding the Maastricht treaty. Crucially, sustainable development also provides a cause and programme for Europe on the world stage, providing a constructive counterpoint to the unbalanced 'free trade' orthodoxy of the USA and promoting multi-lateral cooperation (as with the Kyoto accords on climate change)." Read more [6]

Want to argue for or against Sustainable Europe?
Email `openEuropa@openDemocracy.net`
or post on the discussion board [1]

Competitive Europe

This is a vision of an economically competitive Europe, with open markets leading to widespread prosperity—but it is usually advocated only as part of a European framework of social market regulation.

Peter Sutherland [7], ex-Commissioner & chairman of BP: "In Europe we have a much greater belief in a social system. In general we have higher taxation as a percentage of GDP—it is a different model to that of the United States. And we have regulatory mechanisms that avoid the abuse of dominant positions, such as our Competition Directorate, currently run by the very active and efficient Mario Monti.

"All of this fits in with the model I would espouse. It has elements of the liberal economic agenda, more competition and the opening up of economies to create efficiency and innovation, and yet it adds political mechanisms which ensure that the system is not abused, and that its product is distributed effectively and efficiently... I personally would like a direct community tax system in the EU to support the institutions and those who are deprived." Read more [7]

Want to argue for or against Competitive Europe?
Email openEuropa@openDemocracy.net
or post on the discussion board [1]

Social Europe

There are many different versions of this vision of social Europe based on solidarity. They range from Peter Sutherland's idea of tamed competitiveness (above) to Pierre Bourdieu's radicalism.

Pierre Bourdieu [8], sociologist: "Some of the instruments for the politics which is needed are to be found at the European level (at least to the extent that European institutions and businesses can have a causal effect on the dominant forces of the world stage). It follows that the construction of a unified Social Europe, capable of bringing together the different forces in all their divisions, as much in the national arenas as in the international, is the priority of all those who wish to resist effectively the dominant forces of our time...

"Solidarity is the tacit moving force behind the greater part of their activities... In addition to the development and coordination of new social movements and the willingness to work at a European level, it is also important to renew the more traditional area of trade unions."
Read more [8]

Want to argue for or against Social Europe?
Email openEuropa@openDemocracy.net
or post on the discussion board [1]

Café Europe

Timberlake Wertenbaker [9], playwright: "Cafés mark European differences: a French café is different from a Bulgarian one—for me it's the inimitable smell of a café crème in one and the darkness of the chocolate cakes in the other—but the similarities are stronger: people are sitting around talking, watching, or just reading a paper; it's part of city life, the give and take of a world at ease with itself, and which wants to communicate with itself...

"Of course cafés can be irritating: you get jostled, bumped, so many different conversations and languages can give you a headache, your bag might get stolen, and sometimes you can't find a table because there are too many people. But isn't that better than looking down from the battlements in fear and solitude? I don't want to be imprisoned in the silence of Fortress Europe. Let me walk out into the pavements and sit somewhere, maybe to talk about history, maybe just to watch a city teeming with stories, interest, languages and cultures. Let's not build high, expensive and hostile towers, let's put up instead with the noise, the life, the annoyance, the openness and the music of our Café Europe." Read more [9]

Want to argue for or against Café Europe?
Email openEuropa@openDemocracy.net
or post on the discussion board [1]

Safe Fortress Europe

"Fortress Europe" is used often in the negative. But for many Europeans a safe haven against the chaotic world, keeping out migrants, terrorists, cheap imports or insecurities, is greatly to be desired. French farmer-activist José Bové advocates "food security," one version of this vision of a protected Europe.

Timberlake Wertenbaker [9], playwright: "When I hear the expression Fortress Europe, I shiver. We build fortresses against enemy invaders, fortresses are besieged and people die of starvation and disease, fortresses are stormed, people put to the sword, the women raped. All the gruesome illustrations of my childhood history books come hurtling back in my imagination. Why are we suggesting we build such a place, this Fortress Europe? What hordes of barbarians are galloping towards us? ...

"Fortress Europe means of course, fortress western Europe. Many of the asylum seekers are Europeans themselves, but not part of the EU. Fortress Europe, a besieged castle of pure western Europeans protected by Brussels. Obviously this is a definition of Europe that appeals to some." Read more [9]

Want to argue for or against a Safe Fortress Europe?
Email openEuropa@openDemocracy.net
or post on the discussion board [1]

Europe of Nation-States

Many critics of the process of "ever-closer Union" rally around the idea of the nation-state as the only guarantee of democratic governance, and propose that powers should be repatriated to member states' governments or parliaments.

Jens-Peter Bonde [10], MEP: "Where you can govern efficiently from the national parliament, why then leave the decision to a higher level? You can coordinate and cooperate and do a lot of other good things together internationally. But as much legislation as possible should rest with the democracies, with the voters...

"We say, the catalogue of laws has to be decided by the national parliaments. The national parliaments decide where they can't legislate efficiently on their own; where we need proper legislation for cross-border areas. And they should invite the commission to propose that legislation." Read more [10]

Want to argue for or against a Europe of Nation-States?
Email openEuropa@openDemocracy.net
or post on the discussion board [1]

European Democracy

Visions of European Democracy involve a radical democratisation of European governance, opening up Brussels decision-making to democratic participation, deliberation, election or referendum, and connecting it better either directly to the people or indirectly via representatives.

Kirsty Hughes [11], ex-senior Commission official: "In Brussels, the patronising view is often heard that if only the public understood the EU better, they would support the EU and its institutions much more. The opposite may well be true; if the public had a better view of its inter- and intra-institutional wrangles and machinations, they might well be seriously appalled.

"The hope for a bolder stance on democratic change lies with the Convention members—not with its chairman, nor with the member states. They are in a position to propose substantive democratisation of the Commission, full opening of the Council in legislative mode, greater involvement of national parliaments and more participative democracy.

"But even if the Convention does move in this direction, there remains a risk that it will focus on a small range of institutional reforms and not on genuine participation... The institutions need to recognise that strategies to promote communication and debate are a central part of their role. And this means two-way debate, which will include criticism and disagreement, not simply one-way public relations strategy and political spin... Combined with a genuinely clear, sharp new EU constitution, this could represent a huge leap forward in building a real European political and public space." Read more [11]

Want to argue for or against European Democracy?
Email `openEuropa@openDemocracy.net`
or post on the discussion board [1]

Constitution Europe

In 2003, the Convention on the Future of Europe in Brussels will submit a draft European Constitution providing the institutional foundation of the future Europe. Here is an excerpt from this ambitious vision, which includes parts of many of the visions mapped here, but also has much in common with the pragmatic, incremental "Real Europe" trajectory.

Will Europe acquire powers to enforce these grand objectives? Will this Constitution be adopted by member states and approved by their people at referenda? Are there alternatives? The debate continues.

European Constitution draft [12]: "Reflecting the will of the peoples and the States of Europe to build a common future, this Constitution establishes a Union [entitled ...], within which the policies of the Member States shall be coordinated, and which shall administer certain common competences on a federal basis.

"The Union shall respect the national identities of its Member States. The Union shall be open to all European States whose peoples share the same values, respect them and are committed to promoting them together.

"The Union is founded on the values of respect for human dignity, liberty, democracy, the rule of law and respect for human rights, values which are common to the Member States. Its aim is a society at peace, through the practice of tolerance, justice and solidarity.

"The Union's aim is to promote peace, its values and the well-being of its peoples. The Union shall work for a Europe of sustainable development based on balanced economic growth and social justice, with a free single market, and economic and monetary union, aiming at full employment and generating high levels of competitiveness and living standards. It shall promote economic and social cohesion, equality between women and men, and environmental and social protection, and shall develop scientific and technological advance including the discovery of space. It shall encourage solidarity between generations and between States, and equal opportunities for all.

"The Union shall constitute an area of freedom, security and justice, in which its shared values are developed and the richness of its cultural diversity is respected.

"In defending Europe's independence and interests, the Union shall seek to advance its values in the wider world. It shall contribute to the sustainable development of the earth, solidarity and mutual respect among peoples, eradication of poverty and protection of children's rights, strict observance of internationally accepted legal commitments, and peace between States.

"The Charter of Fundamental Rights shall be an integral part of the Constitution... The Constitution, and law adopted by the Union Institutions in exercising competences conferred on it by the Constitution, shall have primacy over the law of the Member States...

"The Union shall have competence to coordinate the economic policies of the Member States. The Union shall have competence to define and implement a common foreign and security policy, including the progressive framing of a common defence policy." Read more [12]

Want to argue for or against Constitution Europe?
Email `openEuropa@openDemocracy.net`
or post on the discussion board [1]

Simple Europe

Simple Europe is a vision of Europe doing less better—in this case, focusing on setting simple, generally applicable rules which everyone can agree on, but which provide scope for experimentation and diversity.

Frank Vibert [13], analyst: "Simplicity means that the EU and its structures would focus on the type of government activity where the EU can add value to people's lives. This is generally in the rule-making or regulatory area. More specifically it arises in those cases where rules are needed which reach across the entire union, making it easier for people to do what they want to do in social and geographical settings which are distant and unfamiliar...

"The advantage of a European Union for communication is that it can facilitate extensive exchanges of views across the Union. In particular, it is entirely appropriate for the communication of rules with 'reach', that is rules with sufficient content to be useful everywhere: for example, in the identification of minimum standards.

"We should, however, think much more carefully than the current EU does about where exactly we need rules with 'reach' and accept that there are many areas of public policy where differences are instructive and desirable." Read more [13]

Want to argue for or against Simple Europe?
Email openEuropa@openDemocracy.net
or post on the discussion board [1]

Europe of Regions

Many in Catalonia, Scotland, the Basque Country or Corsica dream of a Europe of Regions, where the nation-state in between regions and Europe starts to wither away. At present, political regionalism is near-invisible in Europe, represented in the Council of Regions talking-shop. The Europe of Regions can be seen most clearly in terms of money, in the European regional development programmes [14].

Want to argue for or against a Europe of Regions?
Email openEuropa@openDemocracy.net
or post on the discussion board [1]

Federal Europe

Federal Europe transposes the national vision of federalism, which has developed in countries like Germany, Switzerland and the USA, to the supranational level. Federalism is a word much battled-over in Europe. It means the distribution of power between a central authority and constituent units.

The Oxford English Dictionary defines federalism a little narrowly, as "that form of government in which two or more states constitute a political unity while remaining more or less independent with regard to their internal affairs." For many critics, the idea of a federal Europe constitutes a European superstate; they see its democratic heritage as irrelevant. Other critics see federalism as an outmoded solution to a national, not supranational, set of problems. According to its advocates, the European Union already wields central authority without the democracy federalism could bring (see Executive Europe).

Want to argue for or against a Federal Europe?
Email openEuropa@openDemocracy.net
or post on the discussion board [1]

Europe's Law, Law's Europe

European Community law in principle takes priority over national law, and the latter must be brought into accordance with the former. This vision of Europe sees European legislation and the European Courts of Justice and Human Rights as providing a supranational source of legal principles and judgments which can constrain and overturn national injustices. National legislators don't always agree.

Want to argue for or against Law's Europe?
Email openEuropa@openDemocracy.net
or post on the discussion board [1]

Executive Europe

This vision of technocratic power wielded by the governments and the Commission is an extension of the present "real Europe" trajectory, without democratic additions.

Jens-Peter Bonde [10], MEP: "I think the compromise in the end will be that Justice & Home Affairs will be supranational, run from the Commission in Brussels by Jose Maria Aznar, who will be the European Prime Minister—he is very keen on the police. Foreign policy and defence will never be supranational, they will be directed by the three or four big states. Blair will be the first President, and Joschka Fischer will be the first Foreign Minister... As in France, you have a prime minister to run all the internal policies (who will be the President of the Commission), and then a Presidential function for international affairs, run by a directorate of the biggest states through the Council and its President."

"This is not federalist, not democratic at all. This model puts the power in the hands of the executives: the governments of the member states and the European Commission... There are no voters in this system. It's a corporate way of governing, strengthening the executive at the cost of the voters... It invites the big nations to push their interests through." Read more [10]

Want to argue for or against Executive Europe?
Email openEuropa@openDemocracy.net
or post on the discussion board [1]

Multi-speed Europe

This vision is one of different groups moving at different speeds within Europe, and (given the co-existence of the EU, the Eurozone and the European Economic Area) is already partly coming true. The radical idea of a Franco-German federation has already been floated: this might take in other countries and form a federal core for Europe.

Mathias Koenig-Archibugi [15]: "I come from a country, Italy, where citizens trust the European Commission more than their own national government, and they trust the European Parliament more than their own national parliament... Countries for which EU legitimacy is less of a problem should be able to increase their political integration within the EU framework, while more Euro-sceptic countries should be able to detach themselves from political union." Read more [15]

Ian Christie & Rebecca Willis [6]: "There is a growing realisation that what we need is not a rigid 'Europe of rules' approach to policy which stresses harmonisation and one-speed development... a huge amount of experimentation is needed right down to the lowest level, and a 'Laboratory Europe' or 'multi-speed' strategy could be the framework in which progress can be secured most effectively. This could point the way towards a more flexible model of integration that moves the EU away from the tired and unhelpful stand-off between traditional top-down integrationists and nationalist sceptics." Read more [6]

Want to argue for or against Multi-speed Europe?
Email openEuropa@openDemocracy.net
or post on the discussion board [1]

Have We Missed A Vision?

Tell us. Send an email to openEuropa@openDemocracy.net.

URLS

[1] www.opendemocracy.net/debates/discussion.jsp?id=3&debateId=51
[2] www.opendemocracy.net/debates/article.jsp?id=3&debateId=51&articleId=354
[3] www.opendemocracy.net/debates/article.jsp?id=3&debateId=51&articleId=347
[4] www.opendemocracy.net/debates/article.jsp?id=3&debateId=51&articleId=348
[5] www.opendemocracy.net/debates/article.jsp?id=6&debateId=27&articleId=278
[6] www.opendemocracy.net/debates/article.jsp?id=3&debateId=51&articleId=371
[7] www.opendemocracy.net/debates/article.jsp?id=6&debateId=28&articleId=264
[8] www.opendemocracy.net/debates/article.jsp?id=6&debateId=27&articleId=283
[9] www.opendemocracy.net/debates/article.jsp?id=10&debateId=36&articleId=304
[10] www.opendemocracy.net/debates/article.jsp?id=3&debateId=51&articleId=1062
[11] www.opendemocracy.net/debates/article.jsp?id=3&debateId=51&articleId=375
[12] european-convention.eu.int
[13] www.opendemocracy.net/debates/article.jsp?id=3&debateId=51&articleId=350
[14] www.doingbusiness.cz/r/article.asp?id=165
[15] www.opendemocracy.net/debates/article.jsp?id=3&debateId=51&articleId=748

An alarm-call for Europe

Reinhard Hesse
26 June 2003

Europe needs movement not respite. Before the European Union summit in Thessaloniki, a magnificent seven of intellectuals—including Jurgen Habermas, Umberto Eco, and Jacques Derrida—affirmed the need for a distinct, compelling vision of the continent's future. In its wake, an influential German voice challenges European civil society to live up to the political responsibilities of a moment that offers many dangers and little time.

A large number of our continent's leaders are fresh from spending an early summer grand tour hopping from one picturesque European setting (St. Petersburg) to another (Evian-les-Bains), culminating in the European summit in the ancient city of Thessaloniki [1]. If the climax of their travels is a reminder that the good old continent is still a favoured gathering-site for the world's big bands and key players to mix summits and circuses, the rest of us are waking up to the sound of a shrill alarm clock sounded by some of Europe's finest intellectuals.

This sound [2] is far from the complacent hum of the diplomatic corridors, nor is it yet another emission of that synthesised trash ridiculing *O When the Saints...* on your mobile phone. No, this one comes straight from the bookshelves, and it is pellucidly clear about the seriousness of its call for "Our Renewal," "a Greater Union" and a "European Foreign Policy," and about the choice it articulates—one no less dramatic than: "Humiliation or Solidarity."

In a joint text [3] published in *Frankfurter Allgemeine Zeitung* and *Libération*, Jürgen Habermas and Jacques Derrida—supported in a series of essays by Umberto Eco (*La Repubblica*), Gianni Vattimo [4] (*La Stampa*), Fernando Savater [5] (*El País*) and Adolf Muschg [6] (*Neue Zürcher Zeitung*)—and assisted by a cry for help on behalf of America's true multilateralists by Richard Rorty [7] (*Süddeutsche Zeitung*)—combine their efforts in a passionate, ringing clarion-call for a dynamic, cohesive, and forward-looking Europe.

Moreover, these intellectuals are not content merely to sign a joint declaration—the way many "old guard" US-'Atlanticists' like Madeleine Albright and James R. Schlesinger did some weeks earlier, in a call [8] for "Renewing the Transatlantic Partnership" (whose character can be judged by its more or less polite request that the US be invited to assist any decision-making on the "finality" of the EU).

Rather, our writers and thinkers attempt to launch a series of intellectual salvos and drop them at the front door of politicians and public opinion alike, at the same time claiming a need and right to throw their weight into the political debate about Europe's future. For, as Habermas and Derrida [9] put it, if an "attractive as well as attracting vision of our future Europe" has not even entered the political agenda yet, "then we as intellectuals have failed."

A Europe that stands still will be run over

These essays [10] need intense debate, and they will doubtless provoke opposition. Perspectives may differ, but their arguments share a number of common denominators, namely:

- the urgent need for a common European policy, based on European values and convictions, especially in international affairs
- the sense that, with EU enlargement imminent and in order to avoid more "letters of eight" [11], or any other given number [12], such a policy should be first developed by a "core" of European states more or less grouped around the "founding six" with others invited to join
- the wish to discuss a European "identity" based less on Brussels institutions than on common experience—one that has overcome national hatreds and rivalries, restrained social division and developed an arsenal of "soft power" [13] in international conflict. With this set of yesterday's achievements—the argument goes— today's uncertainties can be faced and visions for tomorrow envisaged in a spirit of tolerance and multi-voiced political culture and ambition.

As if heeding the call almost as soon as it was uttered, Eurocrats from the six "founding states" declared their commitment to cooperate more closely and save the (constitution-making) European convention from imminent failure. A "core Europe" seemed here already in the making, though less an exclusive performance as the inner of a set of "concentric circles." Yet, even after this, it is too soon for "Europtimists" of all countries to applaud. Common action from the brave six is a defensive manoeuvre rather than a forward step—it comes mainly as a response to quite a strong "No," "Nej" or (in the case of Austria) a "Nein" from at least nine other "old" and "new" member states to any substantial institutional reform that goes beyond the rather meagre and most probably inoperable formula reached at the Nice [14] summit of December 2000.

Now, if you have ever been (as I have) close to the bargaining, bickering and negotiating in the final days or even hours before a European summit decision—such as we expect regarding the European constitution—you could bet your last euro on the result that when the process culminates at the grand concluding summit of December 2003 in Rome there will be...a result. European "soft power" does work within Europe, at least.

But perhaps this result could also turn out to be the one drop that makes the whole barrel of Eurosoup spill over. Time is running out yet for more bureaucratic compromise. If there were even a grain of truth in the assumption Habermas and his colleagues make—that the massive anti-war demonstrations in London, Paris, Berlin, Madrid, Rome and elsewhere on 15 February might be a "signal of the birth of a genuinely European public," then it is safe to predict that this public will not for much longer tolerate an eternal revolving around compromise formulas on how to shield the egotisms of national governments.

After all, the continent's young people, unless they aspire to a career in the ever more complicated European administrative apparatus, do not want a common constitution as a set of barriers and exemptions to and from a more unified Europe. They want the will and the rules for clearer, more efficient and more transparent decision making.

Yet even if our philosophers are over-optimistic in respect to the anti-war movement, the idea that one can have "more" Europe by having *less* of it is a treacherous illusion. A Europe of 25 member states (with more [15] to come) that contents itself with being not much more than a common market for national states that pursue a 19th century idea of sovereignty would be not only a missed opportunity; it would be a failure in international politics and, eventually, in economy. And it would rapidly lose public support.

For Europe, there is no future in disunity

Let one country or another opt out of the single currency (it is not hard to think of prominent examples). There may be reasons for that, good or bad, but the national economy will pay the price (or collect the fruit) of such a decision. But if anyone can, by right of veto, opt *all* the others out of a more harmonised taxation system, it is the European economy as a whole that will suffer. Now, the common market with easy access to goods, services and infrastructures in all the member countries is one of the major assets that secure popular support for the EU. The demand here is for *fewer* regulations and *more* comparability, not the opposite.

The same goes for free travel. Already, "Schengeners" [16] feel mildly uneasy if they travel to an "opt-out" destination and have to show their long-forgotten passports again. Without progress in that field, the dangers of international terrorism and other security risks mean that there will be mounting pressure from non-Schengen states, in and outside Europe; in that event, the odds are that Schengen would not be able to survive for long.

But it is, of course, the question of a common foreign policy [17] that pitches the highest notes in the European cacophony. There are four points to make on this vital matter.

First, it is not yet proven that divergences of European governments over how to deal with the US-inspired war against Iraq were an expression of "different national interests." If these "national" differences exist on a deeply rooted scale then apparently lots of Europeans who voiced their opinions in the polls or on the streets did not decipher them.

As for the German, and, for that matter, the French government, they certainly did not raise their voices against war in Iraq out of national economic interest or ideological principle, be it "pacifism" or "Gaullism" [18]. They were just as little convinced as apparently Colin Powell was, in light of the conversation he allegedly had with Jack Straw before making his fabulous presentation of so-called "evidence" on weapons of mass destruction that could only be disarmed by means of an invasion. Now we must hope, for better or worse, that it is not only these nicely-arranged facts that—in Powell's words—"explode in (the Europeans') faces."

Second, division leads to diminution (and keeping the prerogative of a unanimous vote on foreign policy issues means "division" because no one will adopt an earnest common position if each can obstruct consensus). Perhaps some of our allies in the "new Europe" (of Donald Rumsfeld [19] fame) can now pride themselves that the US will "never forget" what they have done in siding with the coalition attacking Iraq. A piece of good advice to them from one of their western neighbours who heard this tune after 11 September 2001 and "Operation Enduring Freedom" [20]: it is true that this US administration will "never forget"—until you want to have a different opinion, that is.

Third, there are principles at stake here. Multilateralism is not a goal in itself. Multilateral nuclear disarmament is. Non-proliferation is always the second-best choice since it will leave weapons of mass destruction in the hands of those who already have them. An overall preventive polity of shared wealth, fair trade, cultural security and environmental provision is by far preferable over "the silly and costly alternative of war and peace" (Habermas [21]). International legality must be reformed, not dismissed. Europe, "old" and "new" alike, knows what security is about; and it knows what insecurity, unequal relations and domination are about. Those lessons learned must not be withheld from others in a world of growing conflict.

Fourth, if Europe does not get its act together, new alliances are already in the making. That precisely is the eternal mistake of the nation-state apologists. Maybe this US administration thinks it *should* "go it alone" and not have any permanent alliances any more. Maybe this administration is indeed pursuing, as one of Britain's finest intellectuals (and a classically Atlanticist figure), Oxford's David Marquand [22] would have it, a sort of "messianic utopianism"—not to be confused with liberal internationalism. Maybe some of America's European allies are nonetheless convinced you need to follow Rumsfeld and Wolfowitz and cherry-pick your friends along with them. In that case, the others will, no doubt, try to form new alliances, let alone hammer out different "axes."

(And speaking of "axes," evil or not: the world would be a better place without them, be they on a horizontal or a vertical line, in the hereafter. No one is served well by the re-emergence of competing lines of tactical preference: Madrid-Warsaw-London on the one hand, Paris-Berlin-Moscow on the other.)

Of course, it would be foolish, insensible and lacking strategic vision to want to build a Europe "against" the United States. But it would be just as utterly stupid for Europeans not to recognise the need to have good relations with Russia, and the opportunities that lie therein.

So, here's to you, the writers and philosophers who are waking us up with this deafening, necessary alarm-call, and focusing attention where it truly belongs: on our European civil societies. After all, it is within our own lands that we are challenged with the need to solve the burning questions of conviviality and progress in a modern world. Now, mind you, a reassertion of what Europe is about and a common foreign policy does not rule out Spanish *siesta*, English *teatime*, Italian *catenaccio* or, unfortunately, German *Ladenschluss* [23]. But if we don't do what needs to be done now, it will certainly be done to us.

URLS

[1] www.germany-info.org/relaunch/politics/new/pol_EU_constitution_2003.html
[2] www.dw-world.de/engish/0,3367,1433_A_884292_1_A,00.html
[3] www.liberation.com/imprimer.php?Article=114475
[4] www.mediamente.rai.it/mediamentetv/learning/ed_multimediale/english/bibliote/biografi/v/vattimo.htm

[5] www.unesco.org/courier/2001_07/uk/dires.htm
[6] www.verw.ethz.ch/cgi-win/whoShow.exe/ws7?ID=660&lang=engl
[7] www.stanford.edu/~rrorty/
[8] www.csis.org/europe/2003_May_Serfaty.pdf
[9] prelectur.stanford.edu/lecturers/derrida/
[10] www.ephilosopher.com/article473.html
[11] www.radio.cz/en/article/37065
[12] www.rferl.org/nca/features/2003/02/07022003192525.asp
[13] www.ksg.harvard.edu/news/opeds/2003/nye_soft_power_iht_011003.htm
[14] news.bbc.co.uk/1/hi/world/europe/1065323.stm
[15] news.bbc.co.uk/1/hi/world/europe/2574719.stm
[16] europa.eu.int/en/agenda/schengen.html
[17] www.iht.com/articles/100207.html
[18] www.bartleby.com/65/de/deGaulle.html
[19] www.rferl.org/nca/features/2003/06/11062003171320.asp
[20] www.comw.org/pda/0201strangevic.html
[21] www.wikipedia.org/wiki/J%FCrgen_Habermas
[22] www.newstatesman.com/nsqpass.php3?num=10&QryTxt=marquand
[23] www.iht.com/IHT/JS/99/js080599.html

America and Europe

Jeremy Rifkin Petr Mach
21 September 2004

Is America a model or a bad example for Europe? In the ninth of our Letters to Americans series, Czech "Eurosceptic" and presidential adviser, Petr Mach, writes to Jeremy Rifkin, US author of "The European Dream"

Dear Jeremy,

You are an American liberal thinker ("liberal" in the American sense of the word) who admires European society for its support of Kyoto agreements, its love of high taxes, its determination to push through the International Criminal Court, and its passion for subsidising "alternative" sources of energy.

You are not alone.

American liberal intellectuals often consider Europe a sort of liberal paradise, or at least a model of what other societies might become. They eulogise Europe as a socialist sister of the conservative America.

But do you really believe that the policies of European governments fairly reflect the wishes of ordinary people? The wishes of ordinary

Europeans are very similar to those of ordinary Americans. Everybody wants to pay lower taxes and to be subject to fewer regulations. But European governments do not enact their citizens' will. There is less freedom in Europe than in the United States—and ordinary Europeans are not happy about it!

You may object that, like America, European countries are democracies, and that government policy always reflects the attitudes of the public. In fact, ordinary Europeans have less influence on government policies than ordinary Americans exercise on theirs. Come to think of it, maybe that is precisely what many American intellectuals admire about Europe!

European governments influence public opinion with state-run television, and use taxpayers' money to influence the outcome of elections. Most national legislation is decreed by the European Union bureaucracy, instead of being subject to the votes of democratically elected parliaments. In short, the admired European "welfare state" relies on government interference with media and a stronger role for bureaucracy in the legislative process.

As an American, you may find these assertions exaggerated. So let me explain in more detail.

On television: European governments run the major national media. The main TV stations are owned by the state ("public service" or "public law" broadcasting in European newspeak). The European model is supported by a lobby of left-wing intellectuals on the boards of these stations. Imagine a public TV channel in America, financed by taxpayers' money, in which people like Michael Moore have the main say; if the average American watched such a channel for one hour a day, maybe then Americans would favour high taxes, the Kyoto protocol, the International Criminal Court, and oppose the Iraq war.

European intellectuals make self-interested claims that their television must not be privatised and that fair competition must not be allowed. Without public broadcasting, they say, people would watch tabloid "commercial" news, biased commentaries and silly "commercial" and "American" movies. You may wish that America had such a powerful public TV channel. Your opinion might then be more influential, but undoubtedly at the expense of American freedom.

On elections: European governments influence elections by campaigning for their own parties. When France held a referendum on whether to keep the franc or replace it with the euro, both the French government and the European Commission spent public money to persuade voters to choose the new currency; opponents of the euro had to rely on limited private funds only.

When the European Union wanted to enlarge eastward—to try to create a "counterbalance" to America, to spread its European "welfare model," and to prevent "harmful" tax competition and "social dumping"—the applicant states held national referenda on EU membership. Governments spent huge sums of taxpayers' money on campaigns in favour of joining, and used public as well as private television stations to convince voters to vote "yes." Would you wish to limit democracy in this way in an effort to make the United States closer to the European model?

On parliaments and laws: the parliaments of European states work differently from the American Congress, where legislation requires majority support. In Europe, most legislation, from environment regulations to tax rates, is passed in the form of "directives;" that is, decrees issued by the institutions of the European Union. These directives prevail over national legislation, so voting on them in national parliaments is just a formality.

Moreover, a country whose parliament fails to pass a directive is likely to face a cut in the subsidies redistributed to it by Brussels, the capital of European bureaucracy. If European countries implement the Kyoto protocol, for instance, it is not because their voters are wiser; it is because they are not consulted. Would you wish the Kyoto accords or high taxes to be legislated in this way in America, too—without the consent of Congress or the state assemblies? American laws would then be more like European ones, but this would certainly be at the expense of American democracy.

In short, the "European model" that European socialist politicians proclaim and liberal Americans admire is not necessarily a model appreciated by ordinary Europeans.

What you admire about Europe are policies influenced by intellectuals and bureaucrats rather than ordinary citizens. As a consequence, what you admire about Europe is its lack of freedom.

Yours sincerely,

Petr Mach

Dear Petr,

I have spent more than one-third of my time in Europe over the past two decades, so I am well aware of the many shortcomings of the European Union that you have outlined in your letter—including the inordinate exercise of top-down power both by governing elites and commercial interests.

But what's particularly interesting is that, these failures notwithstanding, a new generation of Europeans is creating a radical new dream—one that may be better suited than the American dream to meet the challenges of an increasingly interconnected and globalised world in the 21st century. Perhaps our friends in Europe have something to teach us.

Americans love to vacation in Europe. But when we think of institutional Europe, what comes to mind is an old and creaky set of governing machinery riding precariously astride a moribund economy plagued by anti-market bias, inflexible labour policies, bloated welfare bureaucracies, and an aging and pampered population. American policy leaders and economists call it "Eurosclerosis."

But while many Americans dismiss Europe as outdated and out of touch, the reality on the ground—in neighbourhoods and communities, in corporate boardrooms, and in the corridors of power—suggests a far different state of affairs. If the American way of life is over-hyped, Europe's cache has been woefully undervalued and undersold. America is unaware of and unprepared for the vast changes that are quickly transforming Europe from a collection of disparate (and in the past, warring) nations into a United States of Europe.

First, some facts. Most people likely believe that the United States is the world's largest economy. Not true: the European Union's $10.5 trillion GDP eclipses the US by $100 billion. The trade statistics too are revealing: Europe, with 455 million consumers, is now the largest internal market in the world. It's also the largest exporting power. And the euro is now stronger than the dollar—a reality few American economists would have thought conceivable just four years ago.

Americans are so used to thinking of our country as the most successful on earth, they might be surprised to learn that this is far from the case on quality-of-life issues. In the European Union, there are approximately 322 physicians per 100,000 people, compared to 279 in the United States. The average life span in the fifteen most developed EU countries is now 78.2 years, compared to 76.9 years in the United States. The US ranks twenty-sixth among industrial nations in infant mortality, well below the EU average.

Children in twelve European nations now rank higher in mathematics literacy than their American peers, and in eight European countries children outscore Americans in scientific literacy. When it comes to wealth distribution—a crucial measure of a country's ability to deliver on the promise of prosperity—the United States ranks 24th among the industrial nations. All eighteen of the most developed European countries have less income inequality between rich and poor. There are now more poor people living in America than in the sixteen European nations for which data is available.

America is also a more dangerous place to live. The US murder rate is four times higher than that of the European Union. Even more disturbing, the rates of child murder, suicides, and firearms-related deaths in the United States exceed those of the other twenty-five wealthiest nations, including the fourteen wealthiest European countries. Although the United States has only 4% of the world's population, it now contains 25% of the world's entire prison population. While the EU member-states average 85 prisoners per 100,000 people, the US averages an incredible 685 prisoners per 100,000 people.

Europeans often remark that Americans "live to work" while they "work to live." The average paid vacation time in Europe is now six weeks a year. By contrast, Americans receive on average only two weeks. Most Americans would also be shocked to learn that the average commute to work in Europe is less than nineteen minutes. By the standard of what constitutes a better way of life, Europe is beginning to surpass America.

Europe's renaissance is inspired by a new "European Dream," which contrasts in many respects with the older "American Dream." Nowhere is this clearer than over the question of defining the meaning of personal freedom. For Americans, freedom has long been associated with autonomy. If one is autonomous, he or she is not dependent on others or vulnerable to circumstances beyond his or her control. To be autonomous one needs to be propertied. The more wealth one amasses, the more independent one is in the world. One is free by becoming self-reliant and an island unto oneself. With wealth comes exclusivity and with exclusivity comes security.

For Europeans, however, freedom is not found in autonomy but in embeddedness. To be free is to have access to many interdependent relationships. The more communities one can access, the more options one has for living a full and meaningful life. It's *inclusivity* that brings security—belonging, not belongings.

The American dream puts an emphasis on economic growth, personal wealth, and independence; the new European dream focuses more on sustainable development, quality of life, and interdependence.

The American dream pays homage to the work ethic; the European dream is more attuned to leisure.

The American dream is inseparable from the country's religious heritage and deep spiritual faith; the European dream is secular to the core.

The American dream depends on assimilation—we associate success with shedding our former ethnic ties and becoming free agents in the great American melting-pot; the European dream, by contrast, is based on preserving one's cultural identity and living in a multicultural world.

The American dream is wedded to love of country and patriotism; the European dream is more cosmopolitan and less territorial.

The American dream emphasises property rights and civil rights; the European dream concentrates more on social rights and universal human rights.

The American dream encourages willingness to employ military force to protect what we perceive to be our vital self-interests; the European dream entails reluctance to use military force and instead favours diplomacy, economic assistance, and aid to avert conflict, and peacekeeping operations to maintain order.

All this is not to say that Europe has suddenly become a utopia. The point, however, is not whether the Europeans are living up to their dream. We Americans, after all, have never fully lived up to our dream. Rather, what's important is that Europe has articulated a new vision for the future that differs from our own in fundamental ways. These basic differences are crucial to understanding the dynamic that has begun to unfold between the 21st century's two great superpowers.

Jeremy Rifkin

Europe in perplexity

Pierre Rosanvallon

14 July 2004

> An age of globalisation, terrorism, and geopolitical shifts also finds Europe at the end of three great historical cycles. Its thinkers seem bereft of creative, inspiring ideas. Europe, says the French thinker Pierre Rosanvallon, needs to reformulate a new idea of progress in the international order.

Europe's ideological climate has been transformed in recent years, and—contrary to appearances—not only the Iraq war is responsible. The differences that the war revealed between Donald Rumsfeld's notorious "new" and "old" Europe have older and more profound origins. Indeed, the transatlantic divisions [1] that erupted around Iraq had long been a factor in international relations and a marker of growing divergence between western political cultures.

Thus, to understand Europe's condition now requires a longer perspective than Iraq alone provides—one framed by the search for a new European identity after 1989, when the end of the cold war put the rationale and future of the Atlantic alliance in question.

The Iraq war [2], in short, has had an accelerating, polarising and revelatory effect on developments which had already been unfolding for a long period. In doing so it has helped clarify a European intellectual landscape whose new frontlines have emerged from the completion of three great historical cycles.

Three cycles of history

The first cycle rested on the Keynesian model, which since 1945 constituted the horizon of the economic development and social cohesion of European societies. This model reached its end in the 1970s.

The second cycle, arising in political response to the end of the Keynesian period, is the anti-totalitarian movement. This came to an end in 1989 with the fall of the Berlin wall and the collapse of the Soviet bloc.

The third cycle, in reaction to the series of problems (political, economic, strategic) that have arisen since 1989, organises itself around the European project. Today, there are signs that Europe is approaching the end of this third cycle, one that may represent also the end of a distinctively European response to our continent's political problems.

Europe today appears less a solution than the root of a problem. This is why for several years one of the most striking aspects of the European project has been the sort of "defensive intelligence" that guards it.

These contemporary, long-term developments determine the shape of the current European intellectual landscape, but it is the Iraq crisis that has most clearly revealed its contours. Iraq, in brief, has confirmed *the end of the anti-totalitarian moment* that played a central ideological role in the 1970s and 1980s and linked a whole intellectual and political family in the west.

There has been a strong temptation to see in al-Qaida a new form of terrorism capable of reconstituting this old western front. But in Europe the anti-terrorism fight has not given rise, at least for the moment, to a political and intellectual front comparable to 1970s-1980s anti-totalitarianism; and the sharp differences between the successive adversaries (Soviet communism and al-Qaida) make such an outcome unlikely.

Terrorism represents neither an innovative political and social form nor a new type of state regime. Terrorist action links non-political behaviour (nihilist destruction) and a culture of resentment; it "connects" with the other in an insanely violent way, and is not bound to the formulation of any utopia or any project of self-construction.

The Iraq crisis, too, has accelerated the emergence of new (or revived) reactionary ideologies. These are founded on fears and constructs linked in particular to the west's relationship with Islam, which appears in this case as the core problem of which terrorism is only the most visible and dramatic expression.

These reactionary ideologies have been manifest in the affirmation of a new fear of multiculturalism. This was highlighted recently in France with the debate about the Islamic veil in schools, where a visibly hardening neo-republican ideology spread beyond its habitual bases and areas of influence. This fear of multiculturalism tends to dissolve the classic frontiers between right and left.

Such ideologies are similarly visible in the development of a neo-populism that articulates an opposition between the "rooted nation" or the "majority culture" and the world external to it. This phenomenon coincides quite clearly with the success of the far right: it has become linked more generally to discussions about immigration, the welfare state and social fragmentation. In several European countries these discussion have agitated and compromised centrist political parties.

The revival of "declinism" is a further example of the flourishing of reactionary ideologies. Born at the end of the 19th century, reinforced in the 1920s by the impact of Oswald Spengler [3], today it has acquired renewed vigour and lends its vocabulary to a sceptical questioning of the future.

Alongside these regressive tendencies, the current era of wars and crises has revealed an endemic interest in political theories of exceptionalism. It is notable that in Europe, in being applied to the description of supposedly new forms of domination, these have fuelled the revitalisation of ideologies of the extreme left. Its intellectual partisans denounce capitalism and imperialism not on an economic basis but in terms of an absolute "decisionism," or (as in Giorgio Agamben [4]'s analysis of the biopolitical imprint) as incarnations of radial control.

This tendency is reflected also in the fashionability of Carl Schmitt [5]'s ideas of a state of urgency, and of the attractions of a new philosophy of action. Giorgio Agamben, Alain Badiou [6],

Toni Negri [7], and (with a different emphasis) Peter Sloterdijk [8] can be understood in the perspective of an ambivalence that links their "leftism" to a fascination with chosen mechanisms of political control.

Behind these ideas is the force of a profound emotional current, what might be described as a certain "moment of blame" (as in Pascal Bruckner's 1983 book, *Le sanglot de l'homme blanc / The Sob of the White*

Man). These perspectives do not offer a fresh project for democracy in Europe.

A confused landscape

The key challenge for democratic thinking today, beyond the everyday life of democratic societies, is to combine an analysis of resentment towards the west with a redefinition of north-south relations and international relations. The "politics of human rights," which had been at the core of the anti-totalitarian struggle, cannot itself suffice to organise a democratic vision of international relations.

In the 1990s, the foremost problem of the world community was to articulate human rights and nation-building (as in Kosovo, Afghanistan, East Timor). This remains an important objective. But after 9/11 at latest, it cannot see fundamentalist movements or tyrannical regimes as in effect *perversions* of democratic modernity (as totalitarian regimes often were). Rather, it must understand a complex mosaic of contemporary situations where movements and societies fuelled by resentment are locked into a *contradictory* relationship with modernity.

The modern world, which once understood its divisions as a confrontation between rational models, is now structured by a double schism: a confrontation of passions alongside the questioning of modernity itself.

In the coming months, discussions of the future of Europe and about the entry of Turkey into the European Union will concentrate many of these problems. This will underline the fact that Europe today is above all *perplexed*, uncertain of the paths which it needs to take in order to formulate a new idea of progress and of the international order.

In this regard, the crisis of European-American relations since September 2002 has revealed on the European side one thing above all: the difficulties of Europe in its relationship with *itself*.

URLS

[1] www.opendemocracy.net/debates/article-2-88-997.jsp

[2] www.opendemocracy.net/debates/debate-2-88.jsp
[3] www.fordham.edu/halsall/mod/spengler-decline.html
[4] www.upress.umn.edu/Books/A/agamben_end.html
[5] en.wikipedia.org/wiki/Carl_Schmitt
[6] www.egs.edu/faculty/badiou.html
[7] www.hup.harvard.edu/catalog/HAREMI.html
[8] www.petersloterdijk.net/

Europe's green power

Mats Engström

26 March 2007

> The addition of a serious environmental dimension to the European Union's internal reform and soft-power diplomacy could yet make 2007 a year of vision, says Mats Engström.

By 2020, it was becoming clear that the European Union's climate debate and decisions in 2006-07 had been a turning-point in public awareness and public policy whose effects were to be felt worldwide. The twin summits of that year in Germany—the EU's fiftieth anniversary gathering in Berlin on 24-25 March 2007 [1], and the G8 meeting in Heiligendamm on 6-8 June [2] —were remembered as the moment when Europe registered the importance of the issue and began to lead the world in transforming this understanding into a new dynamic of policy change.

It would take time even for the radical changes of energy and transport policy that Europe initiated then really to improve the situation: a climate system already subjected to so much damage is slow in responding. But the alternative, including larger long-term impacts on sea-level rise and ecosystems, would have been far worse.

The climate announcement embodied in the "Berlin declaration" [3] on 25 March 2007 was modest: "We intend jointly to lead the way in energy policy and climate protection and make our contribution to averting the global threat of climate change." But in including the fight against climate change as one of the tasks for the union—part of the desperate attempt to find a new purpose and future after the European constitution was rejected in referenda in France and the Netherlands in 2005—the European Union regained a momentum that, once more, chimed with humanity's and the planet's needs in the 21st century.

Europe's green path

Manuel Castells [4] had formulated one way forward years before in his trilogy on the "network society." The Spanish sociologist proposed building support for the EU by developing "project identities" around issues important to citizens. This concept was embraced by national governments, although their choices of projects differed according to political priorities. Climate change and protection of eco-systems in general was one area where they could finally agree.

Much had already been done. Environmental policy is a European success story, with the EU leading the world in global negotiations. By 2007, more than 200 directives had already improved waste-water quality, decreased emissions from industries and power plants, encouraged recycling and preserved biological diversity. However, environmental policy had recently lost some momentum, while concern about the competitiveness of European companies moved up the political agenda.

After 2007, Europe stepped up into a new gear. This happened particularly after the elections to the European parliament [5] and a dynamic new commission, both in the vital consolidating year of 2009.

Now, by 2020, European companies are world leaders in green technology. They have found new markets as tougher international competition has reduced traditional jobs in industry and service production. Companies gave added value to their products and services by increasing their eco-efficiency, as they did in other areas to meet competition by moving further up the value chain.

The fear that ambitious environmental policy would harm competitiveness has been proven wrong. It has been more often the other way around. European car manufacturers found themselves in crisis when Japanese companies such as Toyota led the development of cars with low fuel consumption, for example hybrid cars. One reason was that the EU had succumbed to intense lobbying in the 1990s and failed to introduce legislation promoting cars with low CO_2-emissions (which California did and Japanese manufacturers were quick to utilise). In 2007, member-states watered down an excellent commission plan [6] for energy-efficiency. Fortunately, two factors—climate change and the fear of being over-dependent on authoritarian Russia—led policymakers to adopt a far-reaching action program for energy- and eco-efficiency in 2009.

It is not only industry that has become greener since then. Emissions from power plants have been reduced, waste water is cleaner and recycling has improved. It has been more difficult to deal with transport, agriculture and other diffuse sources of pollution. Still, tough legislation, environmental taxes, and better public transport have improved the situation. Intense agriculture, using large amounts of fertilisers and insecticides, has decreased in favour of ecological products.

The reform of the common agricultural policy [7], necessary in worldtrade negotiations and made possible by the French presidential election [8] in 2007, has proved less difficult for farmers than foreseen. In fact, the combination of more ecological forms of production with well known European brands proved a success on world markets. ("A Camembert tastes even better with an eco-label," as the French now say).

Ministers for energy, transport, fisheries and finance have made sustainable development a key component of their policy. The "Cardiff process" of integrating environmental issues, based on the Amsterdam treaty, had started during the British presidency in 1998 but later lost momentum. It was reinvigorated by German chancellor Angela Merkel [9] at the June 2007 summit [10].

Strategic decisions by investors and transnational companies have also contributed to the rapid development of more eco-efficient technology. Developments in the United States encouraged European investors to put more emphasis on the environmental performance of companies. Pension funds and insurance companies were among the first movers.

A global alliance

Many problems remain. In some member-states, implementation of environmental legislation is slow. Globally, some countries are free-riders, not taking on commitments appropriate for their level of economic development. The most significant players have however reached a kind of consensus. The EU, the United States, Japan, China, India, Russia and Brazil still disagree on many issues, but the most turbulent years now seem to have passed.

A number of factors contributed to the progress in global environmental policy. The political and public-policy shifts in the United States were crucial. In 2007, twenty states had signed up to a more ambitious climate policy than the George W Bush administration's position. After the Democrats won the 2008 presidential election, Washington changed its attitude towards binding targets for reducing emissions of greenhouse gases, developed other parts of its environmental policy and subsequently regained its position as a global leader.

The US seemed ready to take on more of its responsibility, and the EU developed efficient measures, such as a better emission-trading system. To begin with, this was not enough to convince others. Negotiations on climate change [11] and other international environmental issues were stalled by rapidly developing countries such as China and India, and by authoritarian oil-rich countries such as Russia and some middle-eastern states.

The situation was further complicated by the *renminbi*-dollar crisis in the early 2010s, when the US introduced trade tariffs on Chinese products and Beijing responded by replacing dollars with euros in its currency reserve, prompting financial convulsions around the globe.

This was the moment when the European Union and its member-states again came into their own—showing leadership by building an alliance with the least developing countries, which also contained the areas most affected by climate change and the degradation of natural resources. The key to success was delivering on promises of increased development assistance, debt reduction and reduced trade barriers. The EU also learned to listen better to the views of developing countries and began to create real partnerships; the example of the Basel convention [12] in the 1990s, where the EU and the G77 group [13] of developing countries worked together to ban exports of dangerous waste from rich to poor countries, was an inspiration. Non-governmental organisations from the north and the south, working more closely together than before, can claim a large part of the credit for this alliance.

The reforms of the World Trade Organisation and the International Monetary Fund in the wake of this period of crisis increased transparency and gave developing countries more influence, which made them in turn more prepared to discuss difficult issues such as trade and the environment. The United Nations created an Economic Security Council [14] to provide more stability to the world economy. One of its primary concerns was to reduce speculation in currencies and commodities. The extremely rapid price fluctuations were halted in favour of long-term investment and human development in poor countries.

Discussions with China became easier as the modernised Communist Party understood it had to take more effective action against water scarcity and land degradation if it was to remain in power and govern well. The reform of state-owned enterprises reduced heavily polluting industry and the building of welfare system provided an occasion to introduce environmental taxes. The latter proved particularly effective after stringent measures against corruption were implemented at last.

India, a regular voice of developing countries, found that it was more difficult to remain in that position when the EU and large parts of the G77 formed alliances. The growing middle-class demanded environmental reforms and was reinforced by a private sector that faced green competition from abroad. When the monsoon rains were drastically reduced for the third year in a row, causing massive problems with food supply, India became a driving force for stronger international agreements against climate change.

Russia was the hardest nut to crack. It was not until the "June revolution" demanded democratic reform and an end to corruption that non-governmental organisations could work freely in Russia and independent media recover its status. The subsequent media exposure of the country's massive environmental and health damage helped build Russian public opinion in favour of radical environmental measures. The cleverly designed climate agreements made it possible for Russian companies to make big profits by energy conservation and reduced emissions, finally convincing the Kremlin too.

The far side

The European Union had been a stronger, shaping influence than before in helping to facilitate these changes. The success of the euro, the coordination of external economic policy and further enlargement all increased its political clout. In 2007, Europe's political leaders had recognised the link between environment and security in an unprecedented way. The security strategy of the EU was given a green dimension. A further beneficial consequence was that later conflicts over water and other resources were analysed more thoroughly, and the understanding of migration flows caused by climate change or depletion of land was integrated within wider environmental and human-security perspectives.

Also in **openDemocracy** on the European Union at fifty:
Aurore Wanlin, The European Union at fifty: a second life [p. 167] (15 March 2007)
Krzysztof Bobinski, European unity: reality and myth [p. 76] (21 March 2007)
Frank Vibert, The European Union in 2057 [p. 173] (22 March 2007)
George Schöpflin, The European Union's troubled birthday [18] (23 March 2007)

When the revived, focused new European constitution [15] finally entered into force, the European Union's foreign policy too could become more effective. A greater role for green diplomacy was one of the results. The previous infighting between the council secretariat and the commission was reduced. The union's could really prove its value by using all of its instruments [16] in trying to convince other of the need to move forward on the environment.

In retrospect, policymakers and many other key players active in the momentous years 2007-09 are owed a debt of gratitude for their farsightedness. In that pivotal period, the much discussed "soft power" of the European Union acquired a new dimension. Europe's green power became an established fact of political life, spreading its influence in the world and increasing the quality of life for its citizens—thus contributing to its own legitimacy.

To promise a more ambitious environmental policy in 2007 and then delivering results was the source of renewal for the EU—not a bad way of celebrating [17] a fiftieth birthday.

URLS

[1] www.eu2007.de/en/News/Press_Releases/March/0325AABerlinDeclaration.html
[2] www.g-8.de/Webs/G8/EN/Homepage/home.html
[3] www.eu2007.de/de/News/download_docs/Maerz/0324-RAA/English.pdf
[4] annenberg.usc.edu/Faculty/Communication/CastellsM.aspx
[5] www.europarl.org.uk/guide/GEPmain.htm
[6] www.rferl.org/featuresarticle/2007/1/F7A61D68-4FC7-453C-B6E8-38F173F01B98.html
[7] www.epha.org/a/495
[8] www.election-politique.com/france.php
[9] www.eu2007.de/en/News/Speeches_Interviews/March/0325BKBerliner.html
[10] www.eu2007.de/en/index.html
[11] europa.eu/50/news/theme/070209_kyoto_en.htm
[12] www.basel.int/
[13] www.g77.org/
[14] www.un.org/aboutun/mainbodies.htm
[15] europa.eu/scadplus/glossary/constitution_en.htm
[16] www.evropa.bg/en/del/europe-a-to-z/eu-institutions.html
[17] europa.eu/50/index_en.htm
[18] www.opendemocracy.net/democracy-europe_constitution/EU_Birthday_4463.jsp

European unity: reality and myth

Krzysztof Bobinski

21 March 2007

A return to the origins of European integration in the 1940s-50s reveals a more complex story than the official celebrations allow, says Krzysztof Bobinski.

Few of today's Europeans looking at a photograph of the event will be able to recognise the twelve politicians who signed [1] the Treaty of Rome on 25 March 1957 which established the European Economic Community (EEC). Konrad Adenauer, the first West German chancellor and post-war icon, will spark some recollection; Joseph Luns (Dutch foreign minister and future Nato secretary-general) and Paul-Henri Spaak (Belgian foreign minister) will be familiar to many of their compatriots; Walter Hallstein [2], the first head of the European commission will be well known to students of European studies. But even these statesmen, and certainly most of their companions, will seem to a modern generation of Europeans anonymous, remote figures from a distant age.

The European Union's grand narrative [3], reflected in many histories of modern Europe, tells it differently. These twelve men are credited with formative achievements: signing a treaty that opened the way to the formation of an organisation in Europe which (at the Berlin summit of 24-25 March 2007 [4]) celebrates its fiftieth anniversary; which, for all the doubts it raises in its (now) twenty-seven member-states, has many countries clamouring to get in; and which—above all—is credited with preserving peace in post-war Europe. In this official version, these twelve men are far-sighted architects of an epic political project.

The EU mythology of the *pères fondateurs* has the great men of Europe staring out across the war-wasted cities and farms of our continent, saying "war — never again!," and committing themselves to European unity [5]. And—*voila!*—the deed was done.

A look at the documents and memoirs of the period paints a more complex picture [6], one which shows that the project was (as today) never an easy one. Why, for example, did these architects of a united Europe take twelve years after the cessation of hostilities in Europe in May 1945 to arrive at Rome? The question suggests another: was it indeed the second world war which gave birth to the European project, or was it rather the cold war?

Stefan Glazer, a Polish diplomat representing the Polish government-in-exile [7], sent a revealing report from Brussels to his superiors in London in May 1945 (two months later, the communist regime was to take over his embassy when the western allies withdrew recognition from the London government). It said that the plans for federation which had been discussed in the early 1940s between exiled governments (Dutch, Czechs, Belgians—including Spaak) now seemed forgotten. Glazer noted that as the war ended, everyone was thinking in terms of bilateral agreements.

Glazer was in a position to know. After all, he had been involved in the wartime talks which saw the exiled government of Wladyslaw Sikorski [8] pressing for a Polish-Czechoslovak federation, as well as federative links with others. The Polish exiled leaders were fully aware that the freedom of countries such as Poland after the war could only be secured through a pooling of sovereignty in larger federal groupings.

The arrival of the Red Army in central Europe in 1944-45 in full chase [9] after the retreating Germans put paid to such ideas. The Soviet Union made it clear to Prague that it didn't want any talk of federations in Europe, especially with the Poles.

But by 1946-47 it was the evolving perception of a Soviet threat to western Europe which gave the cause of European unity the push it needed to get underway. From the late 1940s, it appears that—for all the talk of establishing peace in Europe which undoubtedly did motivate the proponents of European integration—the main driving force behind the European project was the need to rearm the Germans and put them on the frontline of the cold war without alarming the French. And a key role here was played by the Americans [10], who were wholeheartedly behind the plan (with the CIA pouring buckets of money into the European Movement [11] to boot).

Also in **openDemocracy** on the European Union's past, present and future:
Frank Vibert, Absorption capacity': the wrong European debate [p. 108] (21 June 2006)
Aurore Wanlin, Adieu, Europe? [p. 115] (29 June 2006)
Anthony Barnett, The birth of Europe?[19] (9 October 2006)
John Palmer, Germany and Europe: the pull of unity[20] (16 February 2007)
Aurore Wanlin, The European Union at fifty: a second life [p. 167] (15 March 2007)

The reintegration of Germany after the war underpinned the thinking behind the European Coal and Steel Community (ECSC [12]) established in 1951 by Robert Schuman, at the urging of Jean Monnet [13]; and the need to have Germany rearmed but safe for its allies was behind the attempt to establish a European Defence Force (EDF), which faltered in 1954 when the French national assembly failed to ratify the plan. The failure of the EDF was no less a shock then than the failure to ratify the European constitution [14] by France and the Netherlands in 2005. But by then Nato—headed by the Americans—was in place to face the challenge; and there was enough independent momentum in the European project to switch to the construction of a free market in Europe through the Messina conference (1955) and on to the Treaty of Rome.

It is interesting to note that the Messina declaration [15] devotes a lot of space to a common energy policy and the development of nuclear energy, an important current preoccupation for the EU. It is also interesting in the way that the struggle between the integrators and those resistant to further integration continued, then as now, all the time. Indeed, the foreign ministers at Messina only committed themselves to study the issues they set down as aims. Spaak then turned what was presented as a mere study commitment into the draft Rome treaty. This in turn [16] set the basis for a "common market" among the six (France, Italy, Germany, Belgium, the Netherlands, and Luxembourg), which preserved the idea of a body which would look after the common interest of the member-states working together in an EEC on the way to an "ever-closer union."

The people on the stage

What has changed, fifty years on [17]? Well, the Soviet threat has gone and the Americans have lost interest in the European project (indeed, they seem at times to be irritated by it). The Germans are still at the centre of the scheme but fear of that country has much abated. On defence, the project seems to gone full circle as the union once again talks of a defence identity, but this time around wondering who the enemy might be. Indeed the cold war substantially helped the European project [18] by providing a common foe.

What has not changed is that national politicians are still fighting about how far to go down the integration route, with national interests very much at the heart of the debate. But there is a twist: with the onset of referenda as a way of taking decisions in Europe, matters are to an extent out of the national leaders' hands. In a sense it was enough for Paul-Henri Spaak to talk all night to his French opposite number at their hotel in Sicily in 1955 to get the French to accept the need for a common market, when all they initially wanted to agree to was an extension of the ECSC into a number of selected fields. True, they then needed national parliaments to ratify their agreements. Now, whole electorates have to be brought on board. Would the men who brought about the Treaty of Rome have been able to rise to *that* challenge?

URLS

[1] www.historiasiglo20.org/europe/traroma.htm
[2] www.iue.it/ECArchives/EN/WH.shtml
[3] europa.eu/50/index_en.htm
[4] www.eu2007.de/en/Meetings_Calendar/Dates/March/0324-RAA.html
[5] europa.eu/abc/history/index_en.htm
[6] us.penguingroup.com/nf/Book/BookDisplay/0,,0_9781594200656,00.html
[7] www.poland.pl/archives/ww2/article,,id,40832.htm
[8] www.poland.gov.pl/Wladyslaw,Sikorski,%281881-1943%29,1973.html
[9] yalepress.yale.edu/yupbooks/book.asp?isbn=0300078137
[10] www.telegraph.co.uk/news/main.jhtml;sessionid=
RFXOIHUFMLMO3QFIQMFCM5WAVCBQYJVC?xml=/news/2000/09/19/wspy19.xml&
secureRefresh=true&_requestid=7007
[11] www.europeanmovement.org/history.cfm
[12] europa.eu/scadplus/treaties/ecsc_en.htm
[13] www.jean-monnet.net/usmain1.html
[14] europa.eu/scadplus/glossary/constitution_en.htm
[15] www.eu-history.leidenuniv.nl/index.php3?c=52

[16] www.historiasiglo20.org/europe/anteceden2.htm
[17] www.bundesregierung.de/nn_6538/Content/EN/Artikel/2007/03/2007-03-19-bkin-merkel-in-rom__en.html
[18] eubookshop.com/1/187
[19] www.opendemocracy.net/democracy-europe_constitution/european_citizens_3975.jsp
[20] www.opendemocracy.net/democracy-europe_constitution/germany_4356.jsp

Realities

What the European Union is

Simon Berlaymont
23 June 2005

> The European Union bubble has burst. It is time to redefine the European project's core purposes, says insider Simon Berlaymont.

The current affliction of the European Union offers a healthy reminder: don't confuse the symptoms with the disease. The French and Dutch referenda [1] precipitated the crisis, the rancorous Brussels summit that followed embittered it, the cacophonous point-scoring [2] of national governments as the British presidency approaches on 1 July is reinforcing it. But beneath the visible wounds and torments is a European body politic that urgently needs serious, long-term diagnosis and treatment. It is time to redefine what the European Union *is*.

There are many reasons why French and Dutch voters rejected the "treaty establishing a constitution for Europe" in their respective referenda on 29 May and 1 June. Dissatisfaction with current political leaderships, their policies and the results of those policies; anxieties about being in some way swamped by alien forces (Anglo-Saxon liberalism in the case of French voters, big countries in the case of the Dutch) and people (Polish plumbers in France, asylum-seekers in the Netherlands).

No doubt there were other reasons too, some related to the European Union—possibly even some relating to the treaty. Just as unhappy families are all unhappy in different ways, "no" voters express many different fears and resentments (of which a healthy number may be legitimate). This may be a good reason for *not* taking decisions by referenda; but it also exposes the great weakness in the "yes" campaign; that it had no single clear message to counteract the natural bolshiness of the individual citizen.

Also in **openDemocracy** on the future of the European Union:

Krzysztof Bobinski, "Poland's letter to France: please say *oui!*" (May 2005)

John Palmer, "After France: Europe's route from wreckage" (May 2005)

Aurore Wanlin, "European democracy: where now?" (June 2005)

Theo Veenkamp, "Dutch sign on Europe's wall" (June 2005)

The lack of a clear message applies not just to this treaty but to the goals of the European Union itself. In so far as the treaty had a message it was the false one contained in its title: that Europe was acquiring a constitution and was becoming a state. In fact the very ratification process itself—by parliaments in some countries, by referenda in others—tells the real story. This is a treaty and like other treaties it needs to be ratified by the states on whom it confers rights and obligations.

The fact that the treaty was drawn up by a "convention" [3] and that it calls itself (in big print) a "constitution" does not change the reality that it is an intergovernmental document: the title begins with the word "treaty," in small print, but this is what it is. "Constitution" is a part of the excessive rhetoric of Europe [4] that obscures rather than illuminates, and threatens when what is needed is reassurance. The fact that so many countries decided to hold referenda, and the failure of (so far) two of those, owes something to that rhetoric.

What Europe is not

The only clear vision of the European Union comes from the two extreme camps. Paradoxically it is the same, wrong, vision. The federalists' dream/pretence of a European state coincides with the sceptics' nightmare/scare story. Federalists [5] wanted to pretend that that is what they were creating in the "constitution;" sceptics seem to believe that the European state is already with us, and that power and authority has already been sucked out of the nation-states that make up the EU.

Both are wrong: Europe is not a state and is not on the way to being one. It does not have police; it does not run schools; it does not have an army (if Luxembourg felt under threat from Brussels its modest light-infantry battalion would have no trouble seizing the EU headquarters);

it does not even have an army of bureaucrats—the 22,000 who do the business of the EU in Brussels would be about enough for a municipal authority in a medium-sized city.

Europe does of course make laws—which is also what states do; and it is true that in the case of conflict those laws override national law—as is always, necessarily, the case for international law.

But the "it" of Europe is not some alien invader. It is us. The process of making its laws is complicated but the key role belongs to national governments, which have in many cases a formal or an informal veto on the result. The European Commission is a supranational body but in the end it still needs backing from the member-states. The commission's heyday under Jacques Delors [6] was a result not just of Delors's talent and vision, but also of the backing he had from France and Germany (and the marginal role Britain was playing at that time).

For the most part the laws made in Brussels deal with the world of business, including agriculture. For those directly concerned they are often important. But the average citizen knows little of (for example) the third insurance directive. This may contribute (or fail to contribute) to the soundness of the company that sells her insurance, or to the growth of a competitive insurance market across European boundaries so that she can buy her car insurance for Belgium from a London firm, but she is unlikely to notice or in most cases to care.

The things that most people care about—health, education, law and order—are run by national governments and will continue to be so (the "constitution" [7] did not seek to alter that, or much else). In the opinion polls before the May 2005 election, British voters showed little interest in European issues. This was entirely right. In the areas that most voters care most about, Europe is not a major factor.

Even economies are run by national governments. That should be clear from the enormous variety of economic policies in Europe. Levels and systems of taxation vary widely; policies on pensions, state ownership and unemployment are all different. Luxembourg's economy is quite different from that of France; Finland's is different from Greece, Ireland from Germany. It is true that the Stability & Growth Pact (1997 [8]) agreed that its members set some limits on deficits for members of the eurozone, limits which its biggest members have then proceeded to ignore (the probability is that if deficits become really excessive the markets will impose discipline more effectively). Freedom of national action, rather than European constraints, is the most obvious feature of the European economy.

Both pro- and anti-Europeans have oversold the European Union. It does not run economies; it is not a new kind of state. On one level it does not matter much for the everyday life of ordinary citizens; though on another it is very important indeed. But it is dangerous for democracy and dangerous for Europe itself if people do not understand what it really is and what it really does—as the two recent referenda have shown. It would not be a bad thing if those who believe that the European Union is important and useful could tell a single reasonably coherent story [9] about what it is.

What Europe does

The real story is this. The central purpose of the European Union is to enable its member-states to function more effectively. There are four main ways in which it does this.

The first is by creating a big market. Markets, and the division of labour they permit are what makes citizens of modern European states richer than any other people in history; and bigger markets provide a wider division of labour. The European Union helps successful national businesses to escape the confines of a narrow domestic market more easily.

The creation of a single European market [10] allowing free movement of goods, services, investment and people is the origin of most European legislation. Markets need to be regulated. Most national markets began with kings establishing fixed weights and measures; later, regulation (like the Factory Acts [11] in Britain) was introduced to protect workers.

There are differences of opinion about how far regulation needs to go; but a single market requires some level of common standards. This is an area where there are many arguments and scare stories—vital ones because how a market is regulated is critical to its success—and in the case of labour markets it is important for people's lives. So these are significant questions but the area covered is still limited.

The second thing that the EU provides for its member-states is more influence in the world. This is most visible in trade negotiations where the EU is now well established as more or less the equal [12] of the United States. If European countries want to deal on equal terms with the US today, and China and India tomorrow, they need to stick together. No European country on its own will ever get much leverage.

The EU is attempting to pursue this logic in foreign and security, as well as trade, policy. This is more difficult but it is necessary. Bosnia in the 1990s and Iraq since 2002 have shown how ineffective European countries are when they are divided. But when they are united they can make a difference: without Europe there would be no Kyoto Protocol [13], no International Criminal Court [14] and it is now Europe that takes the primary responsibility for peace in the Balkans.

The third contribution the European Union makes seems more abstract but is no less critical. It provides a framework of law [15] and cooperation for its members. Law is needed for many parts of the single market, to deal with management of borders, to protect the environment; cooperation is needed in areas such as the campaign against terrorism and foreign and security policy. To make any of this function some sense of a common enterprise, of mutual solidarity is needed. This has grown up gradually over the years. For a long time the EU has been helped because Germany has been a net contributor of solidarity. Now, sixty years after the second world war this (non-monetary) burden needs to be shared more evenly.

The most important by-product of all this has been peace. This was and is the fundamental reason for the EU; and the by-product is also the strategic objective. Peace is not the natural condition of Europe. For most of their history European countries have been at war with each other. The sixty years of peace since 1945 is a historically unprecedented period. The European Union, which has created common interests and a common framework of law and negotiation has also helped create and sustain the longest era of peace in our history.

Talk of pooling sovereignty is mistaken. No one talks of the United Nations or the World Trade Organisation as a threat to sovereignty, though all states accept the authority of the UN Security Council. European states remain sovereign; but instead of expressing their sovereignty through armies or heavily guarded frontiers they make it felt around the negotiating table. Men are freer, not less free, when they live in a community of law. States are not less sovereign when they create a world of law for themselves, rather than settling their differences by violence.

The fourth achievement of the European Union, and an astonishing one, is that it has succeeded in extending [16] its community of law and democracy more widely into central Europe. The transformation of the countries of east-central Europe into stable democracies and market economies is without precedent. Revolutions normally bring violence and authoritarian rulers (Lenin, Pol Pot or Ayatollah Khomeini). That this did not happen in east-central Europe owes something to support from the EU and to the prospect of membership that the EU offered (Nato was also an important factor but probably less important than the EU).

It may be that this smooth transition misled some in the US into believing that democracy followed automatically on the fall of dictators; Iraq shows this to be false. Central Europe shows what a difference it can make if there is a community of democracies close at hand and able to help. The best hope for the Balkans is now to use the attraction of EU membership to restore security and decent standards of government. Enlargement [17] and the effect it has had is a historic advance that matches the liberation of the post-1989 period. There is something slightly tragic about European citizens rejecting what has been one of Europe's finer hours.

What Europe should be

In none of these four areas does Europe replace the national state. In fact Europe is able to function precisely because it has strong, well-functioning national states (and the states themselves function better because of the European framework). Businesses benefit from bigger markets, citizens from travel without visas, jobs without work permits. Above all, and always forgotten, everyone benefits from a peaceful continent governed by law and negotiation.

The European bubble has now burst. Like the dotcom bubble people got an exaggerated idea of a dynamic, and projected trends past the point of common sense. But though the market in Europe has crashed it does not mean that the whole idea is mistaken. There are, after all, some good technology companies too.

There is no reason why people should love Brussels. The negotiating process is tedious and the results unlovely. The institutions are in many ways a mess and some of the common policies could be improved too. In historical terms the EU is new and still has lots to sort out. But it would be nice if more people had at least a vague idea of what it was and what it does. National governments and Brussels officials could start the process by being a bit clearer in their own minds and a bit more modest in the story they tell.

What is difficult to convey is that although the European Union is not a big or a dominating structure it is still very important. This is often true of institutions [18]. The difference between being democratic and being merely bureaucratic is vital though it is not expressed in large budgets or numbers of officials or visible powers. Whether a state is isolated or whether it lives with other states in a community of law is vital in shaping the character of a state and the way it relates to its citizens. These are things that in the end people come to understand and value almost by instinct, and accept almost as natural—as they do with democracy. Until we get to that point we have a lot of explaining still to do.

Further Links:

Europa-EU gateway: `europa.eu.int/index_en.htm`

Democracy International: democracy-international.org/aboutus.html

news.bbc.co.uk/hi/english/static/in_depth/europe/2001/inside_europe/default.stm

www.unizar.es/euroconstitucion/Home.htm

URLS

[1] democracy-international.org/12.html
[2] www.economist.com/agenda/displayStory.cfm?story_id=4033541
[3] european-convention.eu.int/bienvenue.asp?lang=EN
[4] news.bbc.co.uk/1/hi/in_depth/europe/euro-glossary/default.stm
[5] www.federalunion.org.uk/index.shtml
[6] www.euractiv.com/Article?tcmuri=tcm:29-129770-16&type=Profile
[7] www.unizar.es/euroconstitucion/Home.htm
[8] europa.eu.int/comm/economy_finance/about/activities/sgp/sgp_en.htm
[9] europa.eu.int/abc/index_en.htm
[10] www.politics.co.uk/issues/european-single-market-$2108036.htm
[11] www.bbc.co.uk/history/timelines/britain/vic_indust_growth.shtml
[12] europa.eu.int/comm/external_relations/us/intro/
[13] unfccc.int/essential_background/kyoto_protocol/items/2830.php
[14] www.icc-cpi.int/about.html
[15] en.wikipedia.org/wiki/EU_Law
[16] news.bbc.co.uk/hi/english/static/in_depth/europe/2000/redefining_europe/
[17] www.auswaertiges-amt.de/www/en/eu_politik/vertiefung/erweiterung_html
[18] news.bbc.co.uk/hi/english/static/in_depth/europe/2001/inside_europe/eu_institutions/default.stm

France's 'non', Holland's 'nee', Europe's crisis

Kirsty Hughes
1 June 2005

"The European Union is at a major turning-point. It has attempted, through an unprecedented process of open debate and dialogue, to design a strategic role and direction for itself in the 21st century. For now it has failed." Kirsty Hughes on Europe's crisis of democracy.

The French *non* to the European Union constitution on 29 May is still reverberating across Europe, probably to be followed by a Dutch [1] *nee* on 1 June—tipping the European Union into the biggest crisis in its history [2]. This crisis reflects failures of communication and of democracy; behind them is a third failure, of both politics and imagination—the inability of both France and the EU to come to terms with the historical and geopolitical turning-point of 1989, and to find new roles for themselves in the post-cold war world.

A communications failure

There is no quick fix to deal with the French decision or the ensuing crisis. Beyond the French cabinet reshuffle [3], European politicians have reacted slowly—partly from shock, partly from the lack of any "plan B," and partly because they are waiting for the Dutch to vote on 1 June and, beyond that, for the European Council summit on 16-17 June [4]. But the union looks set for a period of infighting, recrimination, conflict and tension: pulling together in a crisis, even at a time of major global challenge, does not appear to be on the cards.

The French rejectionist camp spanned a host of unlikely bedfellows and the *non* crystallised their diverse concerns: anger against the French government, unemployment, and the perceived "ultra-liberal" slant of the union and constitution; worry over immigration, the loss of French influence in the EU (associated with prospective Turkish membership), and the consequences of the 2004 enlargement to Poland and other ex-communist states.

Also in **openDemocracy**'s "Europe: after the constitution" debate: Patrice de Beer, John Palmer, Dan O'Brien, Krzysztof Bobinski, Gwyn Prins, Neal Ascherson and Frank Vibert draw lessons from the French and Dutch campaigns

This list makes clear that, in their European concerns, the French were not voting primarily against the constitution but in fact against much of the current direction and politics of the European Union. The constitution itself does not change the balance of social and economic goals pursued by the union; member-states, for example, still control their own employment policies (the European employment strategy [5] is merely a comparison of best practice). The detailed negotiations [6] of the constitution endorsed neither the "free market" nor the "social Europe" model.

Both the Nice treaty [7] of December 2000 and the constitution [8] allow the EU to introduce new laws that go in either direction; the exact decision would depend on political agreement among member-states (i.e. on ongoing, "normal" EU politics), not on the constitution itself. The French *oui* campaign failed to communicate this fundamental point.

A democratic failure

Alongside this communication failure lies a much deeper and hard-to-tackle democratic failure [9]. The drafting of the constitution—involving national and European politicians and governments meeting in public—was more democratic than anything in the EU's history (though some may regret now the lack of a communication budget or strategy), and the constitution itself would in fact make the union more democratic and transparent (not least through ensuring ministers make laws in public). But the French public were not impressed. This suggests that a strategy of making an elitist, complex and technocratic institution slightly less so will not impress Europe's citizens.

In short, the European constitutional process was unable to ensure that EU policies were fully discussed, debated and aired in the same way that national politics are. Such a genuine European political "space"—the product of a pluralist European democracy gathering the multiple strands of information, debate and political influence across the union—has been long talked of but never created; in its absence national politicians and media have variously misled, misrepresented or ignored the European dimension.

The French *non* should lead to a renewed discussion of how to build such a pluralist European democracy. The problem is that European politicians and officials who have spent three years attempting to create a more efficient, responsive, accountable European Union are now bereft of ideas.

So, for the moment, the debate is about whether to abandon the constitution entirely, put it on ice (at least until after the French presidential election in 2007) or continue with ratification in the vague hope that the French could change their minds. The latter route—followed by Danes [10] and Irish [11] in earlier treaty ratifications—seems highly improbable in the French case. A prolonged row over the future direction of the European Union seems assured.

Tony Blair, the British prime minister, was quick to claim that the key issues are economic not political, and that the French are in effect in denial on globalisation. This characteristic British insistence on the economic aspects of Europe (when the constitution was essentially political), seems almost guaranteed to provoke French ire and augurs a likely clash between the countries that represent the greatest contrast of views within the European Union. It could probably not be a worse time for the British to take over the union's presidency.

In such circumstances, where is Europe-wide leadership to come from? In principle, Germany could play such a role, but it is engulfed in its own domestic political turmoil; in any case, Germany no longer plays its traditional role of working with the smaller EU countries. The the European Commission under José Manuel Barroso [12] has lost the leadership authority it had in the era of Jacques Delors.

Also by Kirsty Hughes in **openDemocracy**:
"Europe united?" (September 2001)
"US and Europe fall out over terrorism" (February 2002)
"A constitution for Europe: where is the real debate?" (September 2002)

So, in coming months, all the EU's faultlines could reappear in stark form: larger vs smaller countries, rich vs poor, net budget contributors vs recipients, free marketeers vs social-model enthusiasts, integrationists vs inter-governmentalists, pro-US vs anti-US hegemony, older vs newer member-states. Such tensions would make progress on vital economic and social issues—building a common foreign policy [13], reforming the common agricultural policy or moving smoothly ahead with negotiations with Turkey, the Balkans, or even Ukraine—highly improbable.

A period of introspection, stasis and conflict, with national interests to the fore, now seems likely. Only a year after its enlargement by ten countries in May 2004, the EU is clueless about how to operate with a membership of twenty-five states and in a changing global environment. Some have suggested that a "core" Europe could emerge (based presumably around the eurozone [14] or Schengen [15] states).

The discussion of such options, remote as they are, reflects the European Union's deep failure of imagination: the inability to come to terms with the geopolitical transformations of post-1989 Europe. But it is not inconceivable that if the constitutional crisis does turn into a battle over the economic direction of Europe, there could eventually be a split into two antagonistic blocs. It is all a long way from the more comfortable days of the European Economic Community and the looser European Free Trade Association (EFTA [16]) in the 1960s.

The European Union is at a major turning-point. It has attempted, through an unprecedented process of open debate, to design a strategic role and direction for itself in the 21st century. For now it has failed. If it can pick up the pieces and look for new ways to create a genuinely democratic EU [17], that engages with and is responsive to the European public, then it may eventually emerge stronger. But, between French *non* and Dutch *nee*, it looks as if the European project will be on the rocks for some time to come.

Further Links

The EU Constitution: european-convention.eu.int/docs/Treaty/cv00850.en03.pdf

A brief history of the EU: www.unizar.es/euroconstitucion/Home.htm

Yes Campaign: www.yes-campaign.net

No Campaign: www.nocampaign.com

EU website: europa.eu.int

European Voice: www.european-voice.com

EurActiv: www.euractiv.com/

E! Sharp: www.peoplepowerprocess.com/

URLS

[1] www.bloomberg.com/apps/news?pid=10000085&sid=aeBYbIQoLL74&refer=europe
[2] www.evropa.bg/en/del/europe-a-to-z/eu-timeline.html
[3] news.bbc.co.uk/2/hi/europe/4598849.stm
[4] www.eu2005.lu/en/calendrier/2005/06/16conseur/
[5] www.eu-employment-observatory.net/en/ees/
[6] www.unizar.es/euroconstitucion/Treaties/Treaty_Const_Neg.htm
[7] www.cec.org.uk/info/pubs/bbriefs/bb29.htm
[8] news.bbc.co.uk/1/hi/world/europe/2950276.stm
[9] news.bbc.co.uk/1/hi/world/europe/4552937.stm
[10] www.eipa.nl/Eipascope/93/3/4.htm
[11] www.unizar.es/euroconstitucion/Treaties/Treaty_Nice_Rat.htm
[12] www.dehavilland.co.uk/webhost.asp?wci=default&wcp=NationalNewsStoryPage&ItemID=13039711&ServiceID=8&filterid=10&searchid=8
[13] europa.eu.int/comm/external_relations/cfsp/intro/
[14] en.wikipedia.org/wiki/Eurozone
[15] en.wikipedia.org/wiki/Schengen_Treaty
[16] www.efta.int/
[17] fpc.org.uk/topics/europe/

Dutch sign on Europe's wall

Theo Veenkamp

2 June 2005

> The Dutch referendum vote against the European Union constitution demands that Europe's leaders enter a fresh dialogue that addresses their people's "complicated cocktail of mixed feelings," says Theo Veenkamp.

The most remarkable thing about the Dutch vote on the European constitution is not the actual result [1] of the referendum—a decisive vote of 61.6% against the treaty and 38.4% in favour on a 62% turnout—but what it reveals about the febrile condition of Dutch society. What is so disturbing to many in and outside of Holland is that the "no" could have been just as well a "yes"—and the other way around. Again, the Dutch are surprising the world. After "good old Dutch tolerance," now also "good old Dutch stability" seems to have gone out of the window—just like that.

Yet intriguingly, a recent and reliable internet opinion poll [2] in which 150,000 Dutch participated shows a quite different picture, in three respects.

First, it found a strikingly large consensus about the type of society people want to live in: a place that allows you to work for living and not live for working, one with more solidarity than at present, and where newcomers are still welcome as long as they are properly integrated.

Second, it revealed an unexpected, widespread and realistic agreement about the type of world we live in and the new threats and opportunities (both from inside and outside) it presented.

Third, it registered a staggering near-unanimity (85%) about people's lack of confidence in politics and government institutions to deal effectively with these opportunities and threats. (A telling detail: a sizeable majority of the civil servants who participated in the poll shared this view).

The Dutch complex

If you combine these results with those of other recent research, a complex picture of the troubled relationship between the Dutch and their political elite emerges. The Dutch—international traders in goods and services for centuries—have a very long internationalist tradition and have developed over time sensitive antennae for what is really happening "out there." (The difference in the amount of international news in Dutch traditional media—newspapers, radio [3] and television—compared with the United Kingdom is tangible in this respect). It seems as if many Dutch people, today as in our "golden age" [4], develop in a direct and intuitive manner a realistic sense of what is changing and what is still to come in our world, and what these changes might mean.

This would today be an asset, as it has been in the past, if it were not for the fundamental change that has occurred in the relationship between the Dutch and their government.

Also by Theo Veenkamp in **openDemocracy**:
"People Flow: migration in Europe" (May 2003) (co-author)
"After tolerance" (November 2004)

The widespread support for the post-second world war national social contract—to rebuild the country and create wealth and opportunity for its people—has withered away because (paradoxically enough) the project was completed successfully.

For Dutch citizens, this "success" contains many elements, emotional as well as material. Among others, it means: living in one of the wealthiest and best-organised countries in the world; being relatively happy; living increasingly hectic lifestyles that involve struggling with time to maintain wealth and participate in the good life; discovering that new sacrifices are necessary in order to maintain a trimmed welfare state; worrying about the future of the economy in a globalising word; worrying about growing ethnic pockets of poverty and isolation in the metropolitan areas; worrying about decreasing security [5] ; experiencing a gradual slipping away of control over one's life; becoming more and more anxious about the world in which one's children and grandchildren will grow up.

This complicated cocktail of mixed feeling is topped up with an equally complicated attitude towards the ruling establishment. On one side, sky-high demands on what the government should do to tackle the risks and grab the opportunities; on the other, almost total lack of confidence in the ability of the government to deliver.

It was this potentially explosive mix that was first skilfully tapped by Pim Fortuyn [6], the flamboyant publicist-turned-politician slain in May 2002; it is this same mix that produces so much volatility in voting behaviour on the European constitution in one of the founding nations of the European Union.

A union of diversities

Despite the referendum outcome, a large majority of people in the Netherlands still favours European integration. But their lack of confidence in both Dutch and European political institutions makes many uncertain how to vote. In addition, many feel that European developments are just going too fast. These factors combine with people's uncertainty about the future of the next generations [7] to increase their sense of losing control.

The idea of a "European Democratic Observatory" is elaborated in Theo Veenkamp, Tom Bentley and Alessandra Buonfino, Toward a new European Commonwealth [10], in *The Democratic Papers: talking about democracy in Europe and beyond* British Council [11], Brussels, 2004)

Many politicians in Holland now blame themselves and their predecessors for not having educated their electorates on the meaning of European integration [8] and what is happening in Brussels, but I doubt whether that would have made a large difference to the referendum outcome. The fermenting undercurrent of perceptions and feelings looking for political articulation seems too deeply rooted for that.

In the end the European Union can only be as strong as are the democracies of its member-states. France and the Netherlands can be seen to show that referenda are a powerful impulse to unruly democratic engagement. But the feelings and perceptions articulated through their campaigns reveal a profound gap between voters and political elites that is worrying for the future political stability of these countries and therefore of their democracies.

Each country within the European Union has its own specific history and political culture. But I am convinced that below these visible differences European citizens are already more united than we think in our anxieties and hopes. We all live in a transitional time that is difficult to understand. For affluent and indigent alike, old certainties are disappearing as rapidly as new uncertainties are emerging. The basic instinct of many ordinary citizens all over the expanding Europe—that what we gain by new policies, laws and regulations is being offset by what we lose in other ways—is a sound one and it should be taken very seriously.

Many all over the world are impressed by the European project and tell us how unique and inspiring we are. We, however, find ourselves only just at the beginning of an agonising reappraisal [9]. The deep division of opinion revealed in France and the Netherlands is a clear sign of the fact that the European constitution has become the symbol both of a powerful dream and of an equally powerful conviction that the dream can never be realised if we continue as planned.

Five steps to Europe's future

In this sense, the French and Dutch referenda results are a sign on Europe's wall. They could lead to a substantial decrease of confidence in the European project, inside and outside Europe, with unwelcome consequences that include the stagnation and loss of direction of the European project itself. In other words, this is a major crisis for the European Union.

But it would be disastrous if the EU reacts to the crisis in its usual way: sit it out, talk it through and continue with a watered-down version of its original plans. Such an approach has worked well on many occasions in the past; employed now, it would fail to redress the lack of confidence of the many who have this week uttered either an emphatic "no" or a doubtful "yes."

Every real crisis offers a chance that would never have arisen in more normal circumstances. In this case, the chance is to take some steps—simultaneously backwards and forwards—that together restore confidence, give direction and cater to the imagination of many.

These are five such steps the European Union could now take:

1. first, don't wait too long before "taking your loss" and declaring the constitution dead; the alternative is a long, drawn-out process that waits for the last member-state to decide and allows distrust and stagnation to spread

2. second, decide as soon as possible on the equivalent of a set of "provisional administrative arrangements" for the EU that contain some of the more evident improvements in decision-making that were included in the constitution (and be absolutely clear that "provisional" means just that)

3. third, establish an independent "constitutional laboratory" whose task would be to design a real constitution of (say) ten-to-fifteen pages. This can serve as the foundation document of a European governance arrangement with two elements: it is constituted of strong, stable member-states, and it forms a clear entity of its own that is based on an optimal mix of defined internal and external authority and professional, innovative facilitating instruments. Allow for a period of ten years to develop, decide and implement.

4. fourth, launch a number of initiatives that make absolutely clear what Europe is all about and that will strongly promote the growth of Europe as a living entity. These might include: negotiating a European social contract for sustainable wealth, encouraging a zone of positive interdependence and mutual understanding reaching beyond continental Europe to its neighbouring regions; launching a "European awareness programme" that invites the creation of materials for a new, inclusive European narrative; constructing high-speed rail links between major European cities and their partners to east and south; establishing

a volunteer reconstruction corps, open to qualified young people from all countries, to aid Europe's capacity to resolve conflict and contribute to humanitarian development.

5. fifth, create a "European democratic observatory"—a kind of clearing-house for democratic renewal—to assist in identifying and understanding innovation in democratic practice, and to promote the spread of knowledge and capacity across the wider European region, at all levels of governance. This would be a convincing way of acknowledging the fact that both "old" and "new" democracies in the wider European region are vulnerable and in need of repair, renovation or even reconstruction.

The decisions of people in France and the Netherlands in the referenda on 29 May and 1 June 2005 are not exceptions but true representations of Europeans' current experience of the political institutions and systems that govern them. The results should force us all to stop and think and find new ways to reconnect with each other: those like myself who are in favour of the European constitution, and those many who have lost confidence in the European future currently offered them.

The shared challenge now is find a language that can truthfully address Europe's complicated pattern of thinking and feeling, and from it articulate a European dream that can one day lead to a document that opens with three mighty words: "We, the people ...."

Further Links

The EU Constitution: european-convention.eu.int/docs/Treaty/cv00850.en03.pdf

EU Constitution: www.euabc.com/index.phtml?page_id=207

A brief history of the EU: www.unizar.es/euroconstitucion/Home.htm

Yes Campaign: www.yes-campaign.net

No Campaign: www.nocampaign.com

EU website: europa.eu.int

European Voice: www.european-voice.com

EurActiv: www.euractiv.com/

E! Sharp: www.peoplepowerprocess.com/

URLS

[1] www2.rnw.nl/rnw/en/currentaffairs/region/netherlands/ned050601c?view=Standard
[2] www.21minuten.nl/21minuten/index.asp
[3] www2.rnw.nl/rnw/en/currentaffairs/dutchaffairs/
[4] www.hum.uva.nl/ich/object.cfm/objectID=F98F2A75-E985-4AC8-89B38C1B7A5C9A4C
[5] www.newyorker.com/fact/content/?050103fa_fact1
[6] en.wikipedia.org/wiki/Pim_Fortuyn
[7] www.faceoftomorrow.com/amsterdam.asp
[8] www.eu2004.nl/default.asp?CMS_ITEM=
0A40F6C0A9454866B55AFDD02EC7B8C5X1X42820X47
[9] www.opendemocracy.org/articles/View.jsp?id=2560
[10] www.britishcouncil.org/brussels-democraticpapers-toward-a-new-european-commonwealth.pdf
[11] www.britishcouncil.org/brussels-europe-democratic-papers.htm

Democracy in the European Union, more or less

Krzysztof Bobinski

27 July 2005

A month after the French and Dutch people voted "no" to the European Union's constitutional treaty, several bruised but unbowed adherents of the European project gathered in Warsaw to share wounds, examine runes, and draw lessons. Krzysztof Bobinski reports.

Like the survivors of a defeated military campaign, footsoldiers [1] of the "yes" side in the French and Dutch referenda on the European Union's draft constitutional treaty are slowly beginning to regroup and to ask why things went so badly wrong. A number of them assembled in Poland's capital city on 5 July 2005 to assess the landscape after battle.

The seminar was sparked by an **openDemocracy** article by Aurore Wanlin [2], a French researcher at London's Centre for European Reform, which concluded: "a lack of democratic dialogue at the European level is a damaging hole at the heart of the European project."

Krzysztof Bobinski [17] is a former *Financial Times* correspondent in Warsaw who works for the *Unia & Polska* [18] Foundation, a pro-European NGO in Poland. He reports in this article on a seminar in Warsaw on 5 July 2005, organised by the Unia & Polska Foundation in cooperation with **openDemocracy** and the Polish weekly magazine *Ozon* [19], on the theme: "Does the European Union need more democracy—and if so how much?" The seminar was held under the auspices of the British presidency of the European Union (July—December 2005) and had the financial support of the Polish foreign ministry; the British, Dutch and French embassies in Warsaw; and the British Council [20]].

Isabel Hilton, editor of **openDemocracy**, chaired the seminar. The other speakers were:
Lena Kolarska-Bobińska (Institute of Public Affairs, Warsaw) [21]
Lousewies van der Laan [22] (Member of the Dutch parliament for the D66 party)
Nadège Ragaru [23] *Institut de Relations Internationales et Stratégiques* (Iris,Paris)
Aurore Wanlin [24] (Centre for European Reform, London)
Anne Mette Vestergaard [25] (Danish Institute for International Studies, Copenhagen)

Lousewies van der Laan [3], a Dutch MP and a leader of the "yes" campaign in her country, described her sobering referendum experience: "we struggled and failed to come up with a convincing one-liner explaining to the man in the street what the European Union can do for him."

> "In the Netherlands there was no compelling reason to be for and it became respectable to be against—no one believes there will be a war in Europe or that their prosperity will suffer if the EU disappears."

Lousewies van der Laan was scornful in several directions:

- of past and present EU leaders who had constructed the EU's institutions and enlarged the union after 1989 without taking people with them ("voters kept telling us: 'we were never consulted about this'")
- of France and Germany for breaking the stability pact with impunity and thus showing that the big member-states could play by their own rules
- of Valery Giscard d'Estaing for calling the treaty a "constitution," thereby fuelling fears that the EU was turning into a "superstate"
- of those in the "yes" camp who warned of terrible results if people voted "no"
- of the media, which failed to explain the issues in depth
- of the business community, NGOs and trade unions, which kept their heads below the parapet

As a result, said van der Laan, "the 'yes' campaign was left to the politicians, who are unpopular and whom people decided to teach a lesson." The 'no' campaign, meanwhile, was very successful: "it united xenophobia (the extreme right) and left-wing populism (the socialists) with respectable and credible sceptics ('the Protestants')."

The feeling that the European Union had become a costly irrelevance to most Dutch people [p. 94] buried the "yes" campaign by a margin of 62%-38%. Lousewies van der Laan says:

But, van der Laan concluded, "at least the campaign gave us a debate on Europe." The lesson for this former member of the European parliament was that any further steps on integration must include, consult and persuade the people with them—and that means more referenda.

Democracy's test

Aurore Wanlin developed the themes of her **openDemocracy** article [4] by arguing that the European Union's problem was the disconnect between its institutions and European citizens, who don't feel the EU answers their needs. She echoed Lousewies van der Laan's comment that national politicians had too often used the EU's Brussels institutions as scapegoats [5] for their domestic problems. This, along with the surprising lack of basic information about the EU available in the older member-states, has had the cumulative effect of weakening the EU.

Nonetheless, Wanlin made the rare point that the European Union is one of the continent's *more* democratic institutions. The division of powers in the EU is complex with inputs from the European Commission, the twenty-five member-states, the European parliament and the European court of justice; there are multiple layers of accountability, including directly-elected MEPs and indirectly-accountable national governments.

After making the further rare point that the EU is made democratic by its inability to keep a secret, Aurore Wanlin argued that the draft constitutional treaty had three further democratic features:

- it was designed to address the EU's democratic deficit

- it was put together in the most democratic fashion in the EU's history to date (the post-Laeken convention process, multiple open meetings and dialogues)

- it was to be tested in the most democratic way—referenda in ten member-states (and parliamentary votes in the rest).

French fears, Danish dreams

Nadège Ragaru [6] saw the French referendum (which produced a 56%-44% vote against the treaty) as the moment when "the French people discovered the European Union and decided that they didn't like what they saw."

The 29 May vote wasn't "against (then prime minister) Jean-Pierre Raffarin [7], nor a lack of transparency or democracy in the EU, not even against economic reforms. It was about the realisation that France was no longer the centre of the world and the French elite was no longer running the country."

The French, Ragaru said, are wrestling with identity problems, in fear [8] of foreigners and suffering insecurity about losing their jobs. They voted as they did because they felt that democracy in Europe could do little to protect them in the face of globalisation.

Anne Mette Vestergaard [9] said that Denmark would have voted "yes" if its referendum had been held before the French and Dutch—but after it, a "no" vote would have been a certainty.

From the moment Denmark joined the EU in 1973, its people were told about the economic consequences but left in the dark about the political ones, Vestergaard continued; now, after several referenda on European issues, two of which produced "no" votes, the Danes [10] have become (like Spaniards) "euroenthusiastic." The reason, said Vestergaard, is that the Danes' various referenda have forced us to talk about European issues and about the EU—including enlargement, which is popular in Denmark.

Jean Monnet's ghost

Lena Kolarska-Bobińska's impression was that the European Union has a deeper problem: European elites are losing interest in the European project because of enlargement.

> "Elites in western Europe no longer send out signals saying the EU is a good thing. At the same time, in a country like Poland half of the voters don't vote anyway and a third say they don't care what kind of system of government they have."

Kolarska-Bobińska suggested that "we may be approaching a similar situation in western Europe, with people finding they are unable to use democracy as a tool to further their interests?"

A lively discussion echoed Kolarska-Bobińska's doubts about democracy. Nadège Ragaru said that in France too, elites were unhappy about enlargement [11] while the mass media failed to provide information about the new member-states.

Several speakers suggested that Poles [12] were more interested in economic issues (jobs and wages) than in democracy. A democratic debate requires an informed electorate—and that takes time. Jozef Niżnik [13], an academic, believed that the debate on the constitutional treaty had been a "huge misunderstanding"—the media had orchestrated the debate and the people had answered the wrong question.

Niżnik then articulated a conundrum that European Union pioneer Jean Monnet [14] might have sympathised with: "if people had been consulted on the euro or enlargement we wouldn't have had either ... integration is better accomplished by elites but this is now impossible without popular support." Niżnik concluded: "we have too much democracy."

Where next?

If the European project has a future, Aurore Wanlin, Lousewies van der Laan and Nadège Ragaru felt that the key to it lies in education, information, and media. They agreed that schools should teach the EU's history, politics, processes, ideas and institutions; local authorities should make more information available throughout the union in a decentralised way; and the media should report EU issues and feature its personalities and stories more widely.

As the late Warsaw afternoon became shorter, the proposals [15] came faster. Aurore Wanlin demanded that EU institutions must consult and engage in public debate before undertaking major initiatives; Anne Mette Vestergaard said "give people the first and not the last say;" the formidable Lousewies van der Laan offered a detailed wish-list for the European Union's institutions, including referenda on all major EU steps, European Council meetings being held in public, and strengthening of the principle of subsidiarity [16] (devolved decision-making).

Anne Mette Vestergaard suggested that referenda on all integration issues may not be the best way forward, but agreed that only open discussion could get "people on board." In Denmark, government funds are now available to local communities who want to learn about and discuss EU issues.

With this uplifting set of recommendations, Warsaw's battle-hardened survivors of Europe's travails set off in search of that special brand of European Union democracy that only Polish hospitality, conviviality, and vodka can supply.

URLS

[1] www.opendemocracy.net/democracy-europe_constitution/europeanreferendum_2532.jsp
[2] www.cer.org.uk/about/wanlin.html
[3] www.houseofrepresentatives.nl/members_of_parliament/griffie_lfc/kamerdet7774.html#personalia
[4] www.opendemocracy.net/democracy-europe_constitution/EU_NO_2566.jsp
[5] www.opendemocracy.net/democracy-europe_constitution/vote_2556.jsp
[6] www.iris-france.org/pagefr.php3?fichier=fr/cv/cv2&nom=ragaru
[7] en.wikipedia.org/wiki/Jean-Pierre_Raffarin
[8] www.opendemocracy.net/democracy-europe_constitution/article_2492.jsp
[9] www.diis.dk/sw11181.asp
[10] www.jean-jaures.org/NL/185/0205.pdf
[11] www.opendemocracy.net/democracy-europe_constitution/russia_2647.jsp
[12] www.washingtonpost.com/wp-dyn/content/article/2005/07/02/AR2005070200061_pf.html

[13] www.ifispan.waw.pl/~jniznik/
[14] www.jean-monnet.ch/anglais/pMonnet/monnet5.htm
[15] www.opendemocracy.net/democracy-europe_constitution/2577.jsp
[16] www.euabc.com/index.phtml?word_id=879
[17] www.opendemocracy.net/democracy-europefuture/article_1878.jsp
[18] www.unia-polska.pl/index.php?id=13
[19] www.ozon.pl/
[20] www.britishcouncil.org/poland
[21] epc.objectis.net/Centers/Files/15-poland_new.pdf
[22] www.lousewiesvanderlaan.nl/
[23] www.iris-france.org/pagefr.php3?fichier=fr/cv/cv2&nom=ragaru
[24] www.cer.org.uk/about/wanlin.html
[25] www.diis.dk/sw11181.asp

'Absorption capacity': the wrong European debate

Frank Vibert

21 June 2006

The mood of the European Union is one of renewed if fragile optimism. But its politicians still need to choose reality-based argument and language over evasive jargon, says Frank Vibert.

The "no" results in the May-June 2005 referenda in France and the Netherlands on the European Union's proposed constitution were followed by predictable statements that the EU was in a condition of crisis. This crisis was said to be composed of three elements:

- the rejection of the constitution (more strictly, of the treaty establishing the constitution) by a national vote in two key member-states

- the doubts the failed referenda cast over further EU enlargement

- the doubts they cast over the economy—especially the future of the "Lisbon agenda" designed to improve Europe's ability to compete in global markets.

Such "crisis talk" remains a backdrop [1] to much media discussion, and is reinforced by the apparent lack of substance in some of the EU's consultations (such as the European Council meeting to close the Austrian [2] presidency, before Finland assumes the role for the second half of 2006). But the language of crisis was always artificial and overblown. A year on, the EU's mood is beginning to change for the better.

A clearing wind

There are four reasons for optimism about the European Union. First, there are signs of revived economic growth in the EU's two largest economies, Germany and France, suggesting that gloom over Europe's economic prospects has been overdone. In addition, the strong performance of the euro is positioning it as a real alternative to a weak United States dollar; most of the ten accession states which joined [3] the EU in May 2004 aspire to join the eurozone as soon as possible.

True, not all is reason and light in economic policy. Most notably, the French government has been buffeted by waves of street demonstrations and appears paralysed by fear of further mass popular opposition to economic reform; and the reform intentions of the Italian government elected in April 2006 remain to be tested. More broadly, cross-border mergers and acquisitions continue to be sensitive, and from Spain to Poland have provoked charges about resurgent economic "nationalism" [4]. But the other side of the coin is that such long-awaited mergers are starting to happen, and represent a positive sign that the single market is becoming a reality in corporate boardrooms.

Second, while the "pause for reflection" over the future of the rejected constitution has been extended, at least one possible way ahead is beginning to be mapped. This would involve a more focused and practical approach to institutional reform of the EU. It might proceed by selecting some key items [5] of the constitution (such as the idea for a permanent council president, and the installation of an EU foreign minister) and submitting them to governments; they could then be presented for passage by parliament (where governments can rely on their majorities) rather than as elements of an overarching "constitution" that require endorsement by referendum.

Third, enlargement remains on track despite continuing concerns in each relevant area. The accession of Romania and Bulgaria—due in January 2007—is proceeding, subject to a resolution of EU reservations [6] about the integrity of justice and administration in the two countries. The path is becoming more clearly established in the Balkans, again notwithstanding uncertainties over the future constitutional status of Kosovo, the pursuit of suspected war criminal in Serbia, and the evolution of the newly-independent state of Montenegro. The negotiations with Turkey started in October 2005, and are proceeding even amidst tension over the opening [7] of Turkish ports and airports to Cyprus and a more sceptical mood in Turkey itself over the prospect of EU membership (which in any case will not be realised before 2015).

Fourth, there is a sense that the EU is beginning to punch closer to its economic weight in world affairs (through, for example, its dialogue with Iran over Tehran's nuclear-research programmes). More generally, there is a sense of greater receptivity to Europe's views in the US state department and the White House. If a number of informed observers regard American "unilateralism" as on the wane, this is in part a result of the EU's efforts. The meeting [8] of EU leaders with President Bush in Vienna on 21 June 2006—which includes a more confident expression of European thinking over foreign policy—marks a confirmation of this mood change in the transatlantic relationship.

This change in the EU's body-language is still fragile and it is easy enough to identify four potential weak points:

- enlargement: in Turkey and southeast Europe, many obstacles still lie ahead

- institutional change: the orchestration of the next round of treaty change will demand a high degree of political and administrative skill, particularly of the German presidency in the first half of 2007

- economic renewal: the political manoeuvring around the EuroNext/New York Stock Exchange merger suggests that Euronationalism remains alive and kicking

- power projection: the EU's global diplomacy could yet be badly tarnished if the Doha trade round fails amidst accusations of EU agricultural protectionism.

Nonetheless, a strong case can be made for saying that the EU has turned a corner, and that the language of crisis will evaporate in 2007-08 [9]. By then, Jacques Chirac and Tony Blair will have departed,

Silvio Berlusconi will seem like a bad memory, and a new set of relationships can be formed among European political leaders.

A new jargon

Against this background of cautious optimism, an ominous new debate has started around the latest awkward term in the European Union lexicon that conceals as much as it illuminates: "absorption capacity." It is the latest example of the way that Europe's leaders tend to reach [10] for jargon that is both misleading in itself and meaningless to citizens.

The term "absorption capacity" is derived from development economics, where it denotes the "objective" and measurable limits on a country's ability to make effective use of capital from abroad. In current EU discussion, it is being applied to suggest that there are empirical and "objective" limits to what current EU structures can accommodate—and that these limits have been or are close to being reached.

The appropriation of the phrase in EU discussions has been triggered mainly by fear of Turkish accession to the union. Europe's leaders find the phrase doubly useful in this context: it (positively) generalises the issues posed by enlargement beyond that of Turkish membership alone by invoking the putative empirical constraints imposed by EU structures, and thus (negatively) deflects attention from political arguments about whether Turkey "belongs" or would "flood" Europe with immigrants.

The "absorption capacity" phrase has become useful to two distinct (if occasionally overlapping) groups: those who wish to oppose further enlargement (and particularly Turkish accession), and those who wish to fight for new powers for the EU under a banner different from that of the "constitution". The dexterous convenience of the phrase is that it can bring into one debate each of the four elements of potential weakness in the EU's development: enlargement, institutional change, economic renewal and power projection. It carries the implication that only with a further centralisation of powers will the EU be able to enlarge much further, manage its economic policies effectively, or play a full role in world affairs.

The ideas embodied in the term are fallacious, both on a theoretical and practical level. The theoretical basis of the idea that the EU faces problems of "absorption capacity" is borrowed from what is known as "club theory". This focuses on the difficulties any large club has in making decisions and conducting common policies. As the club increases in size, so the argument runs, the more difficulties arise and the more the benefits of club membership become diluted.

This theory is weak in the context of the European Union. Many of the benefits of EU membership flow from following common rules [11], whose value increases as more people subscribe to them. The benefits are "network" benefits that increase with size and not—as the "absorption capacity" model has it—benefits based on sharing out something with a fixed supply.

The idea of "absorption capacity" is also weak as a practical concept. Its alleged relevance to the EU lies in relation to the difficulty the main institutions (commission, parliament and council) would have in reaching good decisions with a larger membership. But such difficulties evaporate if the various EU institutions are examined individually. Each of the institutions already has rules for making decisions that will work with larger memberships, and the Nice treaty [12] (December 2000) has in case limited the future size of the commission and parliament. Across the European Union and in its separate institutions, the quality of decision-making can improve. But this has to be done for the existing membership anyway and the remedies would apply equally to an enlarged membership [13].

In this light, "absorption capacity" is in the context of the EU not just a flawed but a dishonest concept. First, because it refers to supposed empirical limits that have not been defined and have very weak theoretical and practical underpinnings. Second, because politicians can seek to use an apparently objective and "non-political" term to set new barriers [14] to enlargement rather than confronting the political problems enlargement raises with their domestic electorates.

This approach is also remarkably shortsighted. The EU's greatest achievement to date has been to anchor newly democratised and marketised economies in a larger framework of rules and to provide them with incentives against backsliding. This function would be seriously at risk if the "absorption capacity" mentality gained acceptance.

The phrase is also unhelpful and misleading in the context of institutional change. It is indeed the case that Europe's political leaders will one day have to return to the question of how to reform Europe's rules and institutions. But the mantra of "absorption capacity" is deceptive here too. The reality is that the existing treaties remain unintelligible to citizens, unprincipled about organisation, and fail to provide Europe with an evidence-based, rule-making capacity [15] that also reflects what Europe's citizens want.

The debate initiated over "absorption capacity" is a diversion from the European Union's real political problems: enlargement, rethinking its treaty base [16], economic reform, and its role in the world. These can be resolved only if the EU develops a much simpler overall structure that allows for much greater internal diversity. That is the real challenge facing Europe, and the way to guarantee that the current fragile optimism will be made secure.

URLS

[1] www.cfr.org/publication.html?id=8148
[2] www.eu2006.at/en/The_Council_Presidency/index.html
[3] news.bbc.co.uk/1/shared/spl/hi/europe/04/enlarging_europe/html/eu_expansion.stm
[4] www.euractiv.com/en/financial-services/kroes-nationalism-place-cross-border-mergers/article-153438
[5] www.eubusiness.com/topics/Constitution/index_html/highlights
[6] www.swissinfo.org/eng/international/ticker/detail/EU_delays_decision_on_Bulgaria_and_Romania.html?siteSect=143&sid=6723471&cKey=1147793052000
[7] news.bbc.co.uk/1/hi/world/europe/5087108.stm
[8] www.rferl.org/featuresarticle/2006/06/C1957B56-382F-47A4-BBAD-22DCE0430101.html
[9] news.bbc.co.uk/1/hi/world/europe/5085772.stm
[10] www.euractiv.com/en/agenda2004/eu-cements-absorption-capacity-new-stumbling-block-enlargement/article-156179
[11] www.polity.co.uk/book.asp?ref=0745628532
[12] news.bbc.co.uk/1/hi/in_depth/europe/euro-glossary/1230330.stm
[13] europa.eu/pol/enlarg/index_en.htm
[14] www.iht.com/articles/2006/06/19/news/eu.php

[15] www.fnst.org/webcom/show_page.php/_c-1203/_nr-1/i.html
[16] www.evropa.bg/en/del/europe-a-to-z/eu-timeline.html

Adieu, Europe?

Aurore Wanlin

29 June 2006

> The machinery of the European Union has recovered from the shock of the failed French and Dutch referenda, but not the heart that pumps it, says Aurore Wanlin.

When the French and the Dutch voted against the draft European Union constitution in May 2005, many thought this was an unprecedented crisis in Europe's history. One year on, however, little has changed. In Brussels, everything is back to work as usual. Commentators are increasingly inclined to see the talk of a crisis as "overblown and artificial" (Frank Vibert, "'Absorption capacity': the wrong debate," 21 June 2006). Several factors combine to explain this sense of optimism.

For one thing, the turmoil that many of the constitution's [1] supporters predicted in case of a "no" has yet to come. The EU has even taken some significant and difficult decisions over the past months: the opening of accession negotiations with Turkey in October 2005, the agreement of a new budget deal in December, and the qualified decision on a roadmap [2] to Bulgarian and Romanian membership in January 2007. All this, and economic prospects in some of the union's leading economies are finally looking brighter.

These events can plausibly be seen as evidence of a recovery of balance, while current difficulties—such as yet another skirmish between the United Kingdom and other member-states over the budget settlement—do not appear to call the EU's future into question.

A further reason given for feeling cautious optimism is that a consensus is slowly emerging over three possible approaches that might—individually, or in some combination—offer a route out of the current institutional stalemate.

First, national governments are increasingly rallying to the view that the constitution will never be implemented under its current form. Instead, progress can be made by implementing bits of the constitution or other integrative measures (such as the European Defence Agency) on the ground in an informal or semi-formal way.

Second, and in the longer term, some European politicians (such as France's interior minister and likely presidential candidate in 2007, Nicolas Sarkozy) are calling on member-states to sign a new treaty that would incorporate parts of the constitution, then push it through their parliaments by "normal" legislation rather than resorting to referenda.

Third, agreement among European governments is emerging around the "Hampton Court agenda" [3], alternatively called the *Europe des projets*. This involves a short-term focus on concrete issues that are relevant to their citizens' day-to-day lives in an attempt to bring the EU closer to the people. Energy and migration in particular are top of their list.

A choice from this set of pragmatic solutions to Europe's current problems is the only course at present available to the EU. This could be presented as an attractive as well as an essential course of action. But it underestimates both the intricacy and the depth of the constitutional crisis in which the EU remains trapped.

In a dark wood

There is no simple way out of the current institutional stalemate. The constitution rejected in 2005, after all, consisted of a whole range of complex and interrelated compromises that could not be easily renegotiated. Moreover, even if EU governments did prove capable of negotiating a new treaty, the results would be modest. The Dutch and the French in particular would oppose any change that resembled an attempt to reintroduce the constitution through the back door. Some countries, like Ireland, would have to hold a new referendum. This would almost certainly prompt opposition parties in other countries to put pressure on their governments to hold referenda as well.

The same difficulties exist regarding the so-called *Europe des projets*. The successful execution of such projects requires governments to work together effectively. The EU does not lack grand ambitions, but it certainly lacks the means to fulfil them. Over the last ten years or so, member-states have increasingly been reluctant to use the traditional community method that delegates parts of national sovereignty to the EU to fulfil a specific task. By contrast, they have resorted more and more to intergovernmental instruments. This often has the effect of blurring the division of competences between the European and national levels and making it harder for the EU to reach its targets.

A good case in point is the open method of coordination, a flexible but often inefficient tool used to fulfil the Lisbon agenda [4], agreed in 2000 by EU leaders to increase Europe's competitiveness. At the same time, intergovernmental cooperation itself is no panacea: as national governments increasingly seek to defend their national interests and resort to protectionist rhetoric, the relations between them can easily sour.

Waiting for the light

The overall crisis of the EU that is revealed here, however, is not new. It has its roots as far back as the beginning of the 1990s with the Maastricht treaty [5]. The French and Dutch referenda of 2005 were simply a wake-up call. There is no escape from the reality they reveal: that it is likely to be much harder to pursue European integration in the future [6]. There are three main reasons for this.

First, European integration is reaching a stage where it encroaches on core national sovereignty. In the past the EU has worked more or less along the lines of the "bicycle theory" [7]: each new step towards more integration leads to the next one (or "if you don't keep going forward you will fall over"). Creating a single market by getting rid of internal tariffs meant that the EU had to address regulatory barriers. The single market, coupled with the cross-border freedom of capital, led to the single currency. The price of this very success is that the EU has now reached a point where it will be much harder to go forward.

The services directive [8] is the perfect example. It is more difficult to create a single market in services than in goods because it would set national social systems in direct competition. Such a step, though economically sensible, carries high political and social costs. Furthermore, future EU integration would inevitably concern taxation or foreign policy, which are at the core of national sovereignty. The union will have to make sure that it takes the people on board and has the legitimacy to make such steps. Even this may not be enough: governments will also need to think carefully and make sure they give the EU the means to reach its objectives.

A second obstacle to further European integration is enlargement. Enlargement has long provided a motor for further political integration and institutional changes. However, the latest EU enlargement [9], the inclusion of ten new member-states (mainly from eastern and central Europe) in May 2004, created the feeling that the EU was coming closer to its "natural" geographical limit.

Also in **openDemocracy**'s "Europe: after the constitution" [11] debate:
Kirsty Hughes, "France's *non*, Holland's *nee*, Europe's crisis" [12] (1 June 2005)
Mats Engström, "Democracy is hard, but the only way" (6 June 2005)
Simon Berlaymont, "What the European Union is" (23 June 2005)
Ivan Krastev, "The new Europe: respectable populism, clockwork liberalism" (21 March 2006)
John Palmer, "Europe's enlargement problem" (23 May 2006)

This in turn is prompting a feeling that the EU as a political project might be nearing its end. Such a feeling, combined with a leadership vacuum, makes it unlikely that the EU will take any bold new steps towards more integration. There is no shortage of challenges which member-states could address together at the EU level—climate change or energy security are just two—but the political momentum behind the EU project is running out of steam.

A third reason is the combination of falling popular support coupled with the crisis of Europe's nation-states. There is a social malaise in Europe, most evidently in France but not confined to that country. Inequalities are rising significantly, feeding into a growing sense of insecurity and dissatisfaction among the middle classes and a growth in populist forces across Europe. But the EU itself risks being the primary casualty of such a development.

The European Union [10] is nothing outside of its nation-states, unlike nation-states (from Portugal to Poland, Sweden to Slovakia) which have a legal and political existence independently of the EU. The EU is therefore vulnerable on two sides: it needs consistently to justify its *raison d' être* in a way that its member-states do not, while the member-states's democratic and social malaise threatens to weaken the union.

Popular support for the EU has been falling consistently over recent years. Member-states have fed this trend by using the EU as a scapegoat for their own ills and policy failures. Many people have held Europe responsible for the perceived negative impact of globalisation on their daily lives. The EU is viewed as a vehicle for forces such as neo-liberal economics and immigration—even globalisation itself—which many citizens would prefer to keep at bay.

In this difficult political and constitutional—even existential—predicament, the only way forward would be for the EU to find a new sense of direction and show its relevance to its citizens. This remains the European Union's "holy grail." It is more elusive now than ever.

URLS

[1] www.unizar.es/euroconstitucion/Treaties/Treaty_Const.htm
[2] www.euractiv.com/en/enlargement/bulgaria-romania-commission-report-fair-balanced/article-155383
[3] www.euractiv.com/en/agenda2004/hampton-court-summit-go-history/article-146672
[4] www.euractiv.com/en/agenda2004/lisbon-agenda/article-117510
[5] news.bbc.co.uk/1/hi/world/europe/3583801.stm
[6] www.europe2020.org/en/GlobalEurope/GlobalEurope1.htm
[7] www.epp-eu.org/news/newsdetail.php?hoofdmenuID=4&newsID=70&submenuID=49
[8] europa.eu/rapid/pressReleasesAction.do?reference=MEMO/06/222&format=HTML&aged=0&language=EN&guiLanguage=en
[9] news.bbc.co.uk/hi/english/static/in_depth/europe/2000/redefining_europe/default.stm
[10] europa.eu/abc/history/index_en.htm
[11] www.opendemocracy.net/democracy-europe_constitution/debate.jsp
[12] www.opendemocracy.net/articles/View.jsp?id=2560

Bulgaria: the mafia's dance to Europe

Ilija Trojanow
16 August 2006

> A close look at Bulgaria's political institutions casts doubt on the country's fitness to join the European Union in January 2007, says Ilija Trojanow.

Bulgaria is on course to become the twenty-sixth member-state of the European Union on 1 January 2007, when it is scheduled [1] to join along with its northern neighbour Romania. But the current behaviour of its leading power-centres suggests that this southeast European state of 7.7 million people is very far from reaching the EU's institutional norms.

Four elements of Bulgaria's current reality illuminate this predicament: business, organised crime, the legal system, and the police service.

The businessman

Puppets can become dangerous once they start imagining they're pulling the strings and that the money they manage actually belongs to them—when they speak as though they had their own voices and their own brains. Ilya Pavlov was such a puppet.

Pavlov, whose private wealth amounted to an estimated $1.5 billion, was the eighth richest man in eastern Europe. Yet he began his professional life as a wrestler, and a mediocre one at that. A few years later—by riding on the back of the Russian-Bulgarian mafia—he was the proprietor of Multigrup (later MG Corporation), one of Bulgaria's [2] largest corporate groups. Pavlov received decorations from Russia and Israel, and was a frequent guest of former kings and presidents.

At some point, he actually began to believe the role he was playing. He even wanted—he, a puppet!—to act the part of patron. He began appointing Germans, British and Americans to the supervisory board, gradually investing the group's capital in the United States. He detached himself from the mafia networks which had created him in the first place. This, however, was impermissible, for no mafia can tolerate being abandoned by one of its own.

It seems that Ilya Pavlov received signals indicating he was on a hit-list. His fraught position became evident during a state visit to Sofia by Vladimir Putin, when Pavlov managed to force his way into a reception at the Russian embassy with the help of a forged invitation. He took the opportunity to suddenly approach the Russian president, who declined to give him a hearing.

Several days later, when leaving his office surrounded by ten bodyguards, a bullet pierced Ilya Pavlov's heart. That was on 7 March 2003. The country's entire elite was in attendance at the funeral service, the final honour—photographs of the event bear an astonishing resemblance to a scene from a Francis Ford Coppola film. And when he was buried [3] in his home village of Arbanasi in northern Bulgaria, seven bishops—the majority of the nation's holy synod—stood at his graveside. No other Bulgarian had ever been sent off with such fanfare.

The mafia

This contract killing, like all others [4], remained unpunished. Small wonder, for as Zviatko Zvetkov, the former acting chief of the political police, explained to a Bulgarian newspaper: "Contract murder is impossible without the acquiescence or cooperation of the police. As an emanation of the state, the police force is a fixed component of organised crime."

Year after year in Bulgaria, war is declared on the mafia—against its corruption, against weapons—and drug-trafficking, against protection rackets, false credit and fraud of every stripe. And each time, the "war" turns out to be ineffective.

The Bulgarian mafia is a product of the country's totalitarian [5] past. In Sicily, the mafia was formed when the Habsburg imperial powers withdrew and the majority of those previously employed by the army and police became unemployed. In the ensuing period, the mafia became an annex of the state. In countries such as Bulgaria or Russia, by contrast, the power of the mafia was based on the ubiquitous power of the Communist Party and its state security services.

The *nomenklatura* created a parallel shadow economy in order to deal in weapons, drugs and all manner of wares—and most importantly, to earn foreign exchange. With the fall of communism in 1989-90, these structures turned out to be quite useful in converting the nation's misappropriated communal wealth into private capital via a multiplicity of metamorphoses and mutations [6].

If Lenin's proverb that dictatorship is power unchecked by any law is recalled, then it is possible to grasp just how small the *Cosa Nostra* is compared to the many-tentacled Russian mafia. The latter has infiltrated its own society, and is in a position [7] to infect the "old" EU countries as well. The hierarchical structure of Russia's ancient empire, with its centre in Moscow, is mirrored in today's mafia networks—for the umbilical cord has yet to be severed.

The chief prosecutor

Nikola Filchev [8], like most high-ranking representatives of the Bulgarian state, was an employee of the state security services before 1989—and probably of the KGB as well. After the failure of communism, he began by styling himself as an oppositionist; but after the fall of the conservative government of Ivan Kostov [9] in 2001, he began travelling regularly to Moscow.

His stays there were so successful that before long, Putin awarded him a high decoration for special services to the Russian state and presented him with an illustrated and gilded history weighing fifteen kilogrammes, entitled *Russia: Glorious Destiny.*

The ceremony took place in the Russian embassy in Sofia. A somewhat inebriated Filchev rose to recite a poem: "No other country on earth is as powerful as Russia; it is our rock, it is our paragon." Then, with tears in his eyes, he spoke of the common destiny of Russia and Bulgaria, while the numerous uniformed personages in attendance nodded in agreement.

For seven years, from 1999 to 2006, Filchev was responsible for combating crime. During this period, there were hundreds of contract killings, and thousands of dead among the lower ranks of the business community (whether black, grey or white). And how many of these murders did his office solve? None! Not a single mafia boss was ever indicted.

> This article was first published in German in *Die Tageszeitung* [15] on 5 July 2006, and in English by SignandSight [16] on 24 July. This is a slightly edited version of the latter

Nikola Filchev deliberately hindered any investigation that implicated the Russian mafia. After his tenure in office, the opposition demanded his indictment [10] for a variety of crimes. Instead, for his own protection, he was sent as Bulgaria's ambassador to Kazakhstan.

The police service

Bulgaria's conditions [11] for joining the European Union are likely to include more hedge clauses than in the marriage contract between a millionaire and a professional gold-digger. In recent weeks, Europe's governing elites have been tripping over themselves to certify progress [12] in the Balkans. And this despite the fact that the specialists they recently dispatched have returned bearing grave warnings.

In March 2006, Klaus Jansen [13], chairman of Germany's federation of criminal investigators (BDK) was in Bulgaria. He told an interviewer with *24 Tschasa*:

> "I asked about the numbers of officers in terms of age and rank. This tells you whether there are officers working there who have been trained according to up-to-date democratic standards, and how many were already professionally active under the socialist system. This information was classified as secret. All you can do is laugh. I was there in order

to carry out an inspection, and I repeatedly received the reply: that would endanger national security interests. If the EU conveys confidential information to Bulgaria, it will wind up in the hands of criminal organisations."

How are we to explain the sanitised image of Bulgaria that has recently been put on display? For as Klaus Jansen pointedly [14] states: "Beginning in 2007, Bulgaria's problems are going to be my problems."

URLS

[1] www.euractiv.com/en/enlargement/eu-bulgaria-relations/article-129603
[2] www.westcarrollton.org/Bulgaria%20Map.jpg
[3] www.standartnews.com/archive/2003/03/12/english/revelation/s3661_2.htm
[4] www.guardian.co.uk/international/story/0,,1774781,00.html
[5] www.sofiaecho.com/article/todor-zhivkov---the-longest-serving-authoritarian/id_6972/catid_30
[6] www.socialrights.org/spip/article1546.html
[7] www.bdk.de/index.php?option=com_content&task=view&id=668&Itemid=309&mscid=-1
[8] www.online.bg/asp/politicianENG.asp?n1=Nikola&n2=Filchev&n3=Borisov
[9] www.omda.bg/engl/personalia/kostov_engl.htm
[10] www.sofiaecho.com/article/bulgarias-foreign-minister-refuses-to-recall-ambassador-allegedly-involved-in-corruption-scheme/id_16027/catid_27
[11] www.evropa.bg/en/del/eu-and-bulgaria/history-of-relations.html
[12] www.csees.net/?page=news&news_id=55102&country_id
[13] www.sofiaecho.com/article/anti-crime-fight-problems-hinder-bulgarias-eu-accession---jansen/id_16129/catid_66
[14] www.cespolice.org/eng/50217195850e2a61e/54061597c20a3f607.html
[15] www.taz.de/pt/2006/07/05/a0153.1/text
[16] www.signandsight.com/features/867.html

Turkey and the European Union: don't despair

Katinka Barysch

27 November 2006

> The accession of Turkey to the European Union is beset by troubles. It needn't be if both sides concentrate on the positives, the big picture and the long term, says Katinka Barysch.

The relationship between Turkey and the European Union, never easy, has taken a turn for the worse. The dispute over Cyprus—involving Turkey's refusal of access of goods from the (Greek) Republic of Cyprus to its ports and airports, and rejection of compromise proposals involving the opening of the port of Famagusta in the unrecognised Turkish Republic of Northern Cyprus to trade with the EU—is the latest [1] phase of a lengthy period of discontent on both sides.

The breakdown of talks on 27 November 2006 [2] in Tampere, Finland— the current holder of the rotating EU presidency—signals the further entrenchment of this tension. Erkki Tuomioja [3], the Finnish foreign minister, who had hosted separate meetings with his counterparts from Turkey (Abdullah Gül) and Cyprus (George Lillikas), said [4] that the failure to reach agreement would have consequences for Turkey's accession talks; "Business as usual cannot continue."

It is hardly an auspicious sign on the eve of the already controversial [5] visit of Pope Benedict XVI to Turkey from 28-30 November. The pope's visit may not be a European Union matter, but the political background reinforces existing arguments—brought to the fore in the wake of the pope's Regensburg address of 12 September [6] —that religious and historical differences render Turkey and Europe incompatible as long-term partners.

In October 2005, when the European Union started [7] accession talks with Turkey, few could have anticipated such an outcome. The mood then was a mixture of relief, excitement and some apprehension. EU entry was finally in sight. But would Turkey be up to the technical complexities?

Thirteen months on, more than 2,000 Turkish experts and officials are busy with accession [8] preparations. Brussels bureaucrats describe the Turkish team as efficient, focused and committed. The "screening"process, in which Turkish rules are compared with EU requirements, is on course to be completed by the end of 2006. And the reason why Turkey has so far negotiated only one of the thirty-five "chapters"of the *acquis communautaire* [9] is that Cyprus (which entered the EU in May 2004 as part of the enlargement to ten new member-states) is blocking further progress.

Technically, Turkish accession [10] is progressing as well as can be expected. But politically it is in trouble. Excitement has given way to disillusionment on both sides. The EU is concerned about Turkey's slowing reforms and its refusal to honour pledges over Cyprus. Turks are angry that the EU is making politically unacceptable demands, without even being able to guarantee that Turkey will eventually join the EU.

The forthcoming presidential (May 2007) and legislative (November 2007) elections in Turkey, and those next year in key EU states such as France, have raised the political heat even further. If mutual recrimination and incomprehension get worse, Turkey's accession could stall or even fail. Turkey would lose its "anchor" for reforms. The EU would lose credibility and a valuable partner. Both sides need to rethink, and quickly.

Here, then, are three pithy recommendations on the leading areas of concern surrounding the Turkey-EU relationship [11].

EU talks: be constructive!

Turkish politicians need to be constructive and keep their eyes on the big prize: eventual European Union membership. Turks complain a lot about double standards and unfair treatment. The EU is partly to blame: it spends a miserly € 1 million a year on communication in

Turkey—obviously not enough to make Turks understand how enlargement works.

Accession is always tough, not only for Turkey. France under Charles de Gaulle twice (1963, and 1966-67) vetoed [12] Britain's accession. Spain's accession negotiations went nowhere for five long years, as existing members worried about its impact on EU farm policies. Poland was told it would join in 2000—and entered only four years later.

It is true that the enlargement [13] process has changed since the last big round in 2004. But these changes are not necessarily directed against Turkey. Croatia is subject to the same tough criteria as Turkey, but it does not see these conditions as an anti-Croatian plot.

Accession has become tougher, but it has also become more objective. At one time, political judgment was the only measure of progress. Today there are "benchmarks" for each step in the negotiations, and the European commission checks meticulously whether candidate countries implement EU laws. In its strategy report on enlargement issued on 8 November 2006 [14], the commission suggested that the "benchmarks" used in accession negotiations should be made public: a good idea, because this would make it harder for existing member countries to block negotiations on say, competition policy or environmental rules because of disputes over borders or property they have with the candidate in question.

Turks scowl when the likes of Angela Merkel and Wolfgang Schüssel [15] (the German and Austrian chancellors) call for a "privileged partnership" instead of full membership. But Turkey needs to remember that, just like EU-critical remarks coming from Ankara, such calls are primarily meant for home consumption. The fact is that the EU has stuck to its decision to negotiate with Turkey with the objective of full membership.

Europeans will continue to debate whether this is good or bad—as they should in an open, democratic society. Rather than pouncing on pre-election statements in EU capitals or reports by the European parliament [16], the Turkish leadership needs to calm down its voters before support for EU membership drops further.

Cyprus: muddle through!

The division of Cyprus [17] is the most urgent, controversial and convoluted issue on the EU-Turkey agenda. Turkey has committed to extending its customs union with the EU to the new member-states, which involves opening up its ports and airports to ships registered in Cyprus. Ankara now says it will only do so if the Europeans honour their own pledge to open up for trade with Northern Cyprus. But the (Greek) Cypriot government uses its EU veto on the trade question, and some western European politicians say that EU talks should be stopped if Turkey does not open its ports.

Also in **openDemocracy**'s "The future of Turkey" debate:
Reinhard Hesse, "Turkish honey under a German moon" [27] (11 March 2004)
Alex Rondos, "Cyprus: the price of rejection" [28] (22 April 2004)
Murat Belge, "Turkey and Europe: why friendship is welcome" [29] (15 December 2004)
Fred Halliday, "Turkey and the hypocrisies of Europe" [30] (16 December 2004)
Fadi Hakura, "Europe and Turkey: the end of the beginning" [31] (5 October 2005)
Daria Vaisman, "Turkey's restriction, Europe's problem" [32] (29 September 2006)
John Palmer, "A commonwealth for Europe" [33] (11 October 2006)
Fadi Hakura, "Europe and Turkey: sour romance or rugby match?" [34] (13 November 2006)

The news from Tampere on 27 November is the clearest indication that the Finnish government's mediation efforts have gone nowhere. The European commission [18] in early November postponed making a recommendation on whether the negotiations should be—wholly or partly—suspended. But the Brussels summit of EU heads of state and government on 14 December [19] (three days after a foreign-ministers' summit) will have to make or confirm a decision on this.

EU leaders should bear in mind that the Recep Tayyip Erdoğan [20] government has little room for manoeuvre ahead of Turkey's national elections, the first since his moderate Islamist *Adalet ve Kalkınma Partisi* (Justice & Development Party / AKP) came to power in November 2002. Any concessions would play into [21] the hands of Turkey's nationalist opposition. Many Turks feel that, since it was the Greek Cypriots who in 2004 voted down the Kofi Annan plan [22] for reunification (which would have allowed a united Cyprus to enter the EU), it is Nicosia that has to move first.

However important Cyprus is, it is not worth calling off the accession talks over the issue. Turkey would probably be asked to make even bigger concessions before it could resume negotiations. And Cyprus would forego the last chance of having a negotiated settlement.

The best the EU and Turkey can do for now is to muddle through until after the Turkish elections. If Turkey—as still seems likely—refuses to open its ports by the 6 December deadline [23] which the European commission is working towards, Brussels could suspend accession talks on only those chapters that are narrowly related to the customs union. That would not be a disaster, for two reasons. First, Turkey already has a customs union with the EU, so there has already been a lot of progress in many of the areas affected; second, if the EU put part of the negotiations on ice, that would still leave Turkey with twenty-five or thirty other "chapters" to get on with.

In the meantime, the EU should press Cyprus to allow for trade opening. And the Turks should agree to confidence-building measures to prepare the ground for a resumption of United Nations-sponsored talks on reunification.

PR: highlight the positive!

A third issue that is turning the Turks off [24] EU accession is public hostility in western Europe. Fewer than half the citizens in the twenty-five EU member-states want any more EU members, and the prospect of Turkish entry is particularly controversial. In a survey of the "national brands" of thirty-five existing and potential EU member-states, Turkey consistently comes last. More than 80% of Austrians, 60% of Germans [25] and 50% of French people are against Turkish membership, and Austria and France are committed to holding a referendum on Turkish accession.

However, Turks should not be too discouraged by the polls, for three reasons. First, in ten out of twenty-five EU countries, there are more people in favour of Turkish accession than against. Second, opposition to future enlargement is related to economic uncertainties and a more general disillusionment with the EU; but eurozone growth is picking up, and the EU is regaining popularity in many places. Third, these prejudices are superficial and largely based on ignorance.

However, boring government public relations campaigns will not overcome prejudice. What Turkey and the EU [26] need to do is to highlight the positive aspects of the "new Turkey:" the political reforms, which are bringing it closer to the European mainstream; its dynamic economy and increasingly close business links with the EU; its vibrant culture, including food, music and sports; its attractiveness for holidaymakers; and its (hopefully) constructive and professional approach to EU accession. It is still far too early for Turkey and the European Union to give up on each other.

URLS

[1] euobserver.com/?aid=22910
[2] www.eu2006.fi/en_GB/
[3] www.tuomioja.org/index.php?mainAction=showPage&id=9
[4] www.dw-world.de/dw/article/0,2144,2249961,00.html
[5] euobserver.com/9/22955
[6] www.opendemocracy.net/faith-europe_islam/pope_jihad_3914.jsp
[7] www.opendemocracy.net/democracy-turkey/membership_2896.jsp
[8] en.euabc.com/word/8
[9] en.euabc.com/word/12
[10] www.euractiv.com/en/enlargement/eu-turkey-relations/article-129678
[11] www.ibtauris.com/ibtauris/display.asp?K=510000000777820&sf_01=CAUTHOR&st_02=turkey&sf_02=CTITLE&sf_03=KEYWORD&sf_04=VX%5FISBN\%3B\%3D\&m=6\&dc=23
[12] www.sunderland.ac.uk/%7EosOtmc/contem/gaulle.htm
[13] en.euabc.com/word/333
[14] ec.europa.eu/enlargement/key_documents/reports_nov_2006_en.htm
[15] www.eupolitix.com/EN/News/200509/8ce5fdcc-53d2-43a9-8519-858978d33ce8.htm
[16] www.evropa.bg/en/del/europe-a-to-z/additional-information-a-z/additional-eu-institutions/european-parliament.html
[17] www.cyprus-conflict.net/www.cyprus-conflict.net/intro%20page.html
[18] www.evropa.bg/en/del/europe-a-to-z/additional-information-a-z/additional-eu-institutions/european-commission.html
[19] www.eu2006.fi/calendar/vko50/en_GB/1136456998803/?calYear=2006&calMonth=11
[20] www.setimes.com/cocoon/setimes/xhtml/en_GB/infoBios/setimes/resource_centre/bios/erdogan_recep
[21] www.dw-world.de/dw/article/0,2144,2234052,00.html
[22] www.hri.org/docs/annan/
[23] euobserver.com/?aid=22824
[24] www.angus-reid.com/polls/index.cfm/fuseaction/viewItem/itemID/13774
[25] www.angus-reid.com/polls/index.cfm/fuseaction/viewItem/itemID/13788
[26] www.cer.org.uk/turkey_new/index_turkey_new.html
[27] www.opendemocracy.net/arts-Film/article_1784.jsp
[28] www.opendemocracy.net/democracy-turkey/article_1861.jsp

[29] www.opendemocracy.net/archive/barrier2.jsp?redirect=/democracy-turkey/article_2271
[30] www.opendemocracy.net/archive/barrier2.jsp?redirect=/democracy-turkey/article_2271
[31] www.opendemocracy.net/democracy-turkey/membership_2896.jsp
[32] www.opendemocracy.net/democracy-turkey/free_speech_3952.jsp
[33] www.opendemocracy.net/democracy-turkey/european_commonwealth_3985.jsp
[34] www.opendemocracy.net/democracy-turkey/turkey_europe_4088.jsp

Europe's new Ostpolitik: a Polish echo

Ivan Krastev

21 December 2006

> Germany assumes the presidency of the European Union at a time of tension in the EU's relations with Russia. But are Germany's and Europe's interests identical? Ivan Krastev finds the Polish experience of martial law in December 1981 a sobering precedent.

Anna Politkovskaya, the renowned Russian journalist and critic of the Kremlin, was assassinated in Moscow on 7 October 2006. Alexander Litvinenko, a former FSB agent and another foe of the Kremlin, was poisoned in London on 1 November and died twenty-two days later. Russia's defence minister proudly announced that two of the Kremlin's in-house so-called liberals—Vladimir Surkov and Dmitri Kozak—are in fact *siloviki* who either work or used to work for Russia's notorious military intelligence body, the GRU.

Even worse, some film critics even see a resemblance between Russia's president, Vladimir Putin, and the new James Bond: both figures are tough, enigmatic, sentimental and (apparently) ready to quit when the operation is over.

Are these the elements of Russian conspiracy or syndromes of western paranoia? Could James Bond turn out to be a *Russian* spy at the end? More immediately, how should Europe's public make sense of the continent's growing uneasiness about Russia?

Gazprom's [1] combative policy towards European investors, Russia's pressure on Georgia, and the new Kremlin ideology of "sovereign democracy" seem further evidence of the appropriateness of a cold-war framework. What is still unknown is the nature of this cold war: how deep it goes, who is in it, what its prospects are. And if there are traces of nostalgia in its return, is the (formerly) victorious west or the defeated Russians most in its grip—or is it simply that Russia still lives in a cold-war era that the west seems to have forgotten?

One way to address these questions is by posing another: where is central Europe in all this?

The ghost of 13 December 1981

A good vantage-point to consider these pressing issues is Poland. After all, Warsaw's veto on the provisional European Union-Russia framework agreement has established the frontlines in the ongoing German-Polish diplomatic combat over the EU's policy towards Russia. An even more potent Polish dimension lies buried within current disputes, however: the international politics of the crackdown by Poland's then communist authorities on the independent Solidarity trade union on 13 December 1981.

The predominant Polish view of 1981 is that (West) Germany's then *Ostpolitik* —the special concern and engagement with the Soviet-bloc countries to its east—betrayed Solidarity for the sake of maintaining good relations with Moscow. Today, Warsaw sees the new German *Ostpolitik*—symbolised by the Baltic oil pipeline [2] that will bypass Polish territory—as evidence of historical continuity.

Berlin, meanwhile, views Warsaw's hardline position on Russia as a grotesque and insane return to Ronald Reagan's [3] policies towards the Soviet Union in a totally changed post-cold-war environment. While Poland seeks to assert its return to international politics and its readiness to fight for its interests, Berlin tries to persuade east-central Europe that the cold war is gone. The conversation is not going easily.

The historians of the cold war now tend to agree that Afghanistan, not Poland [4], marked the beginning of the end of the Soviet system. "The developments in Poland were a stirring prologue to the narrative of Communism's collapse," writes Tony Judt [5], "but they remained a sideshow. The real story was elsewhere."

The real story *was* probably elsewhere—but it was the crushing of Solidarity, sixteen months after it mushroomed into a national movement following its birth in the Gdansk shipyards in August 1980—that caused the major divide in western policy vis-à-vis the Soviet Union.

For the United States administration of Ronald Reagan (at the end of the president's first year in office), the imposition of martial law in Poland illustrated the weakness [6] of the Soviet system. In two major speeches over the next two years, Reagan insisted that the communist system was tumbling down.

At Westminster in June 1982 [7], he noted as a simple fact that "of all the millions of refugees we've seen in the modern world, their flight is always from, not towards the communist world," and went on to consign Marxism-Leninism to the "trashheap of history." In March 1983 [8], he said that communism is a "sad, bizarre chapter in history, whose last pages even now are being written."

Reagan's policy towards communism was one of economic sanctions, political pressure and war of ideas. In today's terms, it was a policy of regime change justified as a *Moralpolitik*. At the heart of the "Reagan doctrine" were two principles: the rejection of any moral equivalence between the democratic west and the communist east, and of any discussion of the Soviet Union as a normal state with legitimate security interests.

West Germany's perspective on the repression of Solidarity was profoundly different. The announcement of martial law in Poland came at the worst time for the then chancellor, Helmut Schmidt, who found himself in East Germany, on the concluding day of his summit meeting with his communist host, Erich Honecker [9].

Schmidt regretted the developments in Warsaw but insisted that they were an internal Polish affair. Bonn feared destabilisation in Europe and a rise of tensions between the west and the Soviet bloc. Timothy Garton Ash [10] describes the Bonn position of the time thus: as Germans had renounced their claim to national unity for the sake of peace, so the Poles would have to renounce their claim to freedom— in the name of the highest priority... keeping the peace. In short, Reagan's enemy was communism; Germany's enemy was a new war in Europe.

As a result of this clash of perspectives, the crisis of the Soviet bloc in 1981 became the crisis of the western alliance. In most of western

Europe, "Solidarity with Solidarity" was a slogan, but not a policy. As early as February 1982, while Adam Michnik [11],

Jacek Kuroń [12] and their friends languished in prison, Helmut Schmidt sent a high-level personal representative to the government of General Wojciech Jaruzelski [13] to help overcome Poland's "isolation."

No wonder, in 2006, it feels like *déjà vu* all over again. The western alliance is again in crisis over its powerful neighbour to the east. It is tempting to argue, then, that the moment presents a similar choice: freedom-fighters vs *Ostpolitikers*, the politics of principles vs immoral realism.

But seductive arguments are not always valid ones. It may be attractive to depict the current European crisis over its Russia policy as analogous to the crisis of 1981; analogies too, however, can be dangerously misleading.

Europe's new Ostpolitik

The critics of a reunited Germany are right to argue that, as during the cold war, Germany's policy towards Russia is based on neglect of the nature of the regime, a stress on regional stability, and economic cooperation.

On its own account, Berlin's clear unhappiness with recent political developments in Moscow is qualified by three factors:

- Germany is not ready to see Vladimir Putin's Russia (as many others are coming to do) as "Soviet Union lite"
- Germany does not see regime change in Russia as a realistic possibility
- Germany, along with Europe as a whole, are increasingly dependent on Russia's gas and oil.

Germany can thus be blamed for a lack of imagination, but not for a lack of realism. Berlin's decision to treat Gazprom as only a corporate entity, for example, is less hypocrisy or naivety than a statement of hard-nosed realism. Moreover, Germany has stronger arguments than in 1981 in arguing it is engagement not confrontation that can influence internal political changes in Russia.

But a striking feature of the German position is the unwillingness to see any risks and threats for the European Union emanating from Russia's current policies. A disturbing question follows: when it comes to Russia, is the German interest Europe's interest?

The German public opinion that was so sensitive towards Donald Rumsfeld's strategy to divide Europe into "old" and "new" fails to notice that Gazprom is following a similar policy (the only difference is that Rumsfeld was favouring "new Europe" and Russia favours "old Europe"). The danger posed by Russia's policies is of European Union disunity and the failure of the EU project.

Poland's politics of remembering

Poland itself has a different problem. In its attempt to mobilise support for new, Reagan-type, "third-cold-war" policy response, Warsaw fails to notice that Putin's Russia is not the Soviet Union. There are no Russian troops in Prague, Warsaw or Budapest; and while Leonid Brezhnev could not legitimately speak for the peoples of the Soviet Union, Putin can speak for Russia.

Denying Russia its legitimate interests will not allow any meaningful dialogue. The nature of the Soviet threat was very different from the challenge presented by Russia today. Communist ideology, a critical element of the Soviet threat, is gone. By rhetorically fighting the Soviet Union in 1981 the west was fighting communism; by confronting Russia today the west is not confronting an ideological enemy. Poland's attempt to portray Putin's Russia as a modified version of the Soviet Union is unlikely to gain the support of European public opinion.

In short, Europe is not living in a recurrence of December 1981. The choice is not between Reagan-style neo-conservatism and Helmut Schmidt's [14] *Ostpolitik*. The context has changed. (West) German *Ostpolitik* was a strategy of German unification; Germany's new *Ostpolitik* is a politics of unified Germany.

Poland today is also not the Poland of 1981. Then, Solidarity was not so much a representative of the Polish national interest as the symbol of Europe's march towards freedom. Today, official Polish positions are perceived in much of the rest of Europe as unbalanced and counterproductive. The current government of the Kaczynski twins (Lech as president, Jaroslaw as prime minister) is mistrusted by large swathes of the European public, and Poland regarded as a selfish actor in the European Union. The contrast is vivid: the voice of the Polish revolution in December 1981 was stronger than the voice of the Polish government is today.

At the same time, Europe will fail in its Russia policy if it decides to ignore Polish sensitivities. Poland has a point and this point should be heard. The experience of 13 December 1981 convinced Polish society that the nature of a country's regime matters in international relations. The European logic of this Polish understanding is that Europe's Russia policy should start not with a strategic framework between the union and Moscow but with an internal European agreement on the nature of the regime in Moscow.

The Polish experience of 1981 and 2006 is underpinned by the (now) historically rooted sensitivities that the experience of central and eastern Europe has accumulated in the period of transition. "Solidarity Poland" regards Russia today in a similar way as it does "ex-communist Poland;" namely, forces defeated in the cold war only to return as the real winners of the transition.

Both these forces, after all, managed to regain control over the economic levers of rule and over public discourse; to convert intelligence networks into business profits; to close, in the ostensible interest of compromise, the question of historical justice. Russia as a state thus resembles the old communist elites in the former Soviet satellites: economically powerful, capitalist, in love with the manipulative side of democracy, corrupted and corrupting.

Who won the cold war is not an easy question to answer in central and eastern Europe in 2006. The conundrum explains why agreeing on common policy towards Russia will be devilishly hard—and indispensable—for the European Union.

URLS

[1] www.gazprom.com/
[2] www.transneft.ru/Projects/Default.asp?LANG=EN&ID=227
[3] www.whitehouse.gov/history/presidents/rr40.html
[4] www.rferl.org/featuresarticle/2005/08/8b89d311-5067-4c03-9aa6-72500d1f986d.html
[5] us.penguingroup.com/nf/Book/BookDisplay/0,,0_9781594200656,00.html
[6] www.aforcemorepowerful.org/book/excerpts/poland.php
[7] www.heritage.org/Research/Europe/WM106.cfm
[8] teachingamericanhistory.org/library/index.asp?document=961
[9] edition.cnn.com/SPECIALS/cold.war/kbank/profiles/honecker/
[10] yalepress.yale.edu/yupbooks/book.asp?isbn=0300095686
[11] www.dandavidprize.com/laureates/present2006-michnik.html
[12] www.guardian.co.uk/obituaries/story/0,3604,1241458,00.html
[13] edition.cnn.com/SPECIALS/cold.war/kbank/profiles/jaruzelski/
[14] www.theglobalist.com/DBWeb/AuthorBiography.aspx?AuthorId=409

Tony Blair and Europe

Simon Berlaymont

30 May 2007

> Tony Blair came to power in Britain in 1997 promising a fresh era in Britain's often difficult relationship with the European Union. Has the soon-to-depart prime minister succeeded? An experienced writer with extensive professional knowledge of the union's inner workings, Simon Berlaymont, draws up a balance-sheet of achievement and failure.

Among the pro-European majority that lives on the other side of the Channel, Tony Blair is regarded with envy and disappointment. Envy because in spite of everything he is still seen as the most talented and charismatic of European leaders of his time. Like many notable leaders at the end of their term he is more admired abroad than at home. Disappointment because they had hoped for more from the most pro-European British leader anyone will see for some time. And yet both Britain and Europe [1] are different because of Blair, and, in spite of the disappointment, both are the better for him.

The incoming Labour government in 1997 was more European in its outlook than its predecessor. That is no surprise: most new governments arrive determined not to make the mess of Europe their predecessors did. Foreign ministers applauded spontaneously when Lord Carrington set out the new Conservative government's approach in 1979. John Major [2] meant it when he said that he wanted Britain to be at the heart of Europe. But by that time his government was tired and his party divided.

Tony Blair [3] arrived strong and with a modernising agenda that seemed to put Europe at the heart of Britain as much as the other way round. He was the first prime minister from the post-war generation; his memories were not of defending Britain against evil Germans and feckless French. New Labour was built on respect for German social policy and French economic success. He spoke French well and had already established some good relationships on the continent, notably with Helmut Kohl [4]. A positive approach to Europe was part of his party's platform.

A benign rupture

Where did it go wrong? Well, in the first place it didn't all go wrong. Blair leaves behind him one lasting landmark in Europe and many useful achievements.

The latter include a couple of treaty negotiations, Amsterdam [5] and Nice, without the turmoil and angst that had always gone with such occasions in the past—not much of an achievement for anyone else, but for Britain something new.

At Amsterdam it was notable that, rather than fight every comma—the Thatcher/Major practice—Blair was tough on the few issues that mattered, and made deals on the secondary points, behaving, that is, much as other countries do. In passing he dropped the United Kingdom's opt-out from the social chapter, a useful step in the normalisation of the British position in Europe (and one which seems to have passed without any of the terrible results forecast by the Conservative Party).

The summit which finalised the Nice treaty [6] is still remembered as one of the most awful summits of all time, but none of the complaints relate to the British position. It was the awfulness of Nice in fact that persuaded Blair that European institutions needed to be reformed—hence his later espousal of the idea of a permanent chair for the European council.

This also marks Blair off from his predecessors. The normal British approach is to say that there is no need to interfere with European institutions: we should concentrate instead on getting the policy right, reforming the Common Agricultural Policy (CAP) and the like, and let the institutions look after themselves. This has served Britain badly. It fails to recognise that European institutions do need reform: to adjust to enlargement, to reflect the evolution of the union and new priorities—such as crime and terrorism. In the minds of most of its members the EU is a project which remains unfinished and needs to develop further. Prime ministers who do not see this and go into treaty revision negotiations with a purely defensive agenda not only miss the opportunity to shape Europe but give an image of Britain as a grumpy and negative member of the union. At the very least Blair's approach to treaty revision—aided perhaps by the fact that he and Gordon Brown [7] were in the process of revising the UK's constitution at the same time—made him seem more like a normal European.

A litany of progress

A second achievement, big in some ways, small in others, was "the Lisbon agenda." [8] This might be portrayed as Euro-Blairism: putting at the centre of the European agenda the need to reconcile social protection with a dynamic, market-driven economy. This again was an admirable example of Blair behaving as one of his more influential colleagues might have done, using Europe to push his domestic programme. The method by which he tackled this was exemplary: hardly a single colleague was omitted from a series of bilateral summits accompanied by joint initiatives, articles, letters, statements. Everyone was bound in, above all Gerhard Schröder [9] who briefly espoused the *Neue Mitte* as a German version of the Third Way.

The theme was intelligent, the tactics well executed; the trouble is that little was achieved. The European Union has set itself a series of pompous goals—making Europe the most competitive [10] economy in the world by 2010—but there is no evidence of significant changes in any county's domestic policies as a result. The whole process (which still goes on) became bureaucratised and rather *sovietesque* in its setting of targets and quotas, and also in its results. This contrasts for example with the transformative impact of monetary union and the single market.

We might note in passing meanwhile that a radical reform of the CAP [11] has taken place—in which UK pressure over the years has played a part (where have the beef- and butter-mountains gone?) But if you listen to the speeches of UK ministers, including sometimes the prime minister, no one seems to have noticed. Strange: they ought to be hailing it as a triumph for British policy.

The most important collective achievement of the EU during the Blair years has been enlargement. If anything is remembered in European history it is likely to be the EU's achievement in stabilising central and eastern Europe after the end of communism. That Britain played a leading part in this goes without saying: British politicians have always been in favour of enlargement, some with the (mistaken) hope that of a larger and looser union, some to relativise Franco-German dominance, some because it was the only thing they could find to be positive about in Europe. In the case of Blair there is no need to attribute negative motives; in this and in Nato enlargement [12] he was motivated by a strategic vision. Britain played a leading part, as did Germany.

Also on the legacy of Tony Blair in **openDemocracy**:
Roger Scruton, "Tony Blair's genius" (18 December 2006)
Norman Fairclough, "Tony Blair and the language of politics" (20 December 2006)
Felix Blake, "Blair's foreign-policy legacy" (21 December 2006)
Brian Brivati, "The Blair audit: war, human rights, liberalism" (8 January 2007)
Tina Beattie, "Religion in Britain in the Blair era" (10 January 2007)
Tony Curzon Price, "Tony Blair and centralisation" (20 February 2007)
Godfrey Hodgson, "London and Washington: Tony Blair's special relationship" (5 March 2007)

More exceptional is the case of Turkey. Here Britain had a special role in relaunching the idea of Turkish accession (at the Helsinki summit [13] of December 1999), then in keeping it alive, and finally in getting the negotiations started. In the last of these it was the personal stubbornness of Jack Straw that finally won the day.

This was one of the important results of the second UK presidency under Blair. Another was the budget settlement. Some in Europe would probably say that this hardly counts as an achievement since it was the UK that created the obstacle to a deal which it than removed, enabling a settlement. This satisfies the natural preference for blaming others—and the British have been willing victims—but it does not reflect a much more interesting reality.

One part of this is the incendiary nature of European budgetary matters in UK domestic politics. The sensible compromise which Blair proposed, almost certainly against the advice of the chancellor/treasury, leaves both Europe and the UK in good shape. The skilful diplomatic operation that brought the solution about was secretly admired by the Brussels professionals. This was then backed by a bravura Blair presentation in the European parliament in which he argued that the British rebate was the other side of the coin for the way in which the CAP dominated EU spending. The parliament applauded him as enthusiastically as they had earlier when Jean-Claude Juncker [14] attacked him. But it was Blair who solved the problem. It would be nice if, in the UK, this might have laid to rest the idea, stemming from Margaret Thatcher's [15] iconic struggles, that compromise on budgetary matters is always wrong. It is also worth remarking that here as in other areas Blair was part of a pro-European minority in the cabinet (his most solidly pro-European supporters—Peter Mandelson, Charles Clarke and Robin Cook were all gone by then).

The UK presidency was also notable for the useful special summit at Hampton Court, which put energy on the European agenda, at the level where it belongs. The fruits of this will not be apparent for some time to come—energy as well as Europe is a long-term business—but the rewriting of UK energy policy [16] in European terms may (we should hope) be an important part of the Blair legacy.

A new road

The most important bequest is already visible, though like much else remains incomplete. (It is in the nature of things that big changes take time). This is the possibility of a real foreign and security policy for Europe, effectively launched by Blair and Chirac at St Malo in their September 1998 [17] summit. Without a security dimension—the ability to deploy forces—and without the machinery that the deployment of forces requires, namely a standing committee for political consultation, there is no foreign policy.

This was one lesson of Europe's failures in the Balkans in the early 1990s. At that moment Europe found itself facing a security crisis too near to home—both geographically and emotionally—to ignore. Nato was unavailable because the United States was not interested.

"We don't have a dog in that fight," then secretary of state James A Baker [18] was reported to have said. It is also questionable whether Nato would have been able to bring together the political and economic pressures and incentives that were required, in addition to the military. The EU however had no way of deploying military force itself, nor of engaging seriously in political business: monthly meeting of senior officials from capitals are not capable of handling crises.

The Blair/Chirac proposals at St Malo were not just about giving the European Union a rapid-reaction force. They opened the possibility of the EU becoming a real political actor in international affairs. The pre-St Malo situation was well illustrated by the debates on Yugoslavia. These were overwhelmingly about trade preferences—keeping out Yugoslav sour cherries and raspberries—even at a time when the political system there was breaking apart.

Behind foreign policy, ultimately, there always lies the possibility of force [19]. A foreign policy without this possibility is only half a policy, or less. So long as Nato remained the only forum for collective military efforts, and so long as Nato is dominated by the US, European effectiveness and independence in foreign policy would always have limits.

The new road opened by Blair and Chirac leads, potentially, a long way. Not to a Europe which is hostile to the US—this is unthinkable—but to one which is a more integrated and more independent and therefore a better partner for America. The St Malo ideas were embodied in the Nice treaty. Since then the European Union has built up machinery for dealing with political and military questions on a daily basis, including a modest military staff. It has undertaken four military missions, two in the Balkans and two in the Congo—one of these may have prevented serious bloodshed. In addition to this, and not foreseen at St Malo, the EU has also undertaken a whole series of non-military missions in crisis areas including the monitoring of the peace settlement in Aceh and the border crossing at Rafah [20] (between Gaza and Egypt). It is now contemplating the possibility of a major administrative and rule-of-law assistance mission in Kosovo as well as a police-training mission in Afghanistan. In a relatively short time the St Malo initiative [21] has been fruitful in many, often unanticipated ways.

An unwise promise

There is still some way to go before the European Union is capable of taking a place among other continental-scale actors. But these developments are as important in their way as the euro. Any pro-European Briton should be proud of Blair's personal role in them.

Britain being generally a grouchy place, most will probably prefer to remember what they see as Blair's principle sin of omission: the failure to join the euro early in the first term when it seemed as if the prime minister could walk on water and the people would follow him. You cannot be out of the euro and be at the heart of Europe—as Blair always understood. In his own terms therefore, this was a failure. It is nevertheless one we should understand. The previous Labour government collapsed in a series of economic disasters, leaving New Labour [22] with the need to demonstrate financial responsibility. Would it have been wise to risk all on the euro, which was highly contested domestically and which fitted the UK's economic position particularly badly at the moment of decision (at the time the UK was close to overheating and European economies were tending towards recession)?.

Arguably the UK's interest-rate structure (a high proportion of variable-rate mortgage lending) would make it a difficult case at any time. The fact that the UK has prospered outside the eurozone does not make it easier to argue that this was a terrible mistake. The domestic economic success of New Labour has since become a factor against the prime minister's ambitions for Britain in Europe: it is difficult to argue for adopting the euro when the UK economy seems to be doing better than that of the eurozone. And even more difficult to change the psychology in Britain: that we turn to Europe as a remedy for British failure rather than a way to enhance success. If Britain had joined the euro then eurozone interest rates would have been higher by half a point or more over the period; this would not necessarily have been good for other members.

What was a mistake and what does deserve to be criticised was the commitment to a referendum on joining the euro. Clearly a debate would have been needed; and probably it would have been wrong to take such a decision against widespread and determined opposition. But that is what parliament and election campaigns are for. Why should the machinery of monetary policy be subject to a popular vote when less complicated questions such as capital punishment are not? This is a failure in constitutional policy rather than in European policy, but that it should come on these issues illustrates the poisonous nature of the European debate in Britain.

The virus of referenda is contagious. Blair caught it from a weak and divided Conservative Party that needed to avoid the responsibility for taking decisions itself. Later he found himself too weak to resist when they called for a referendum on the constitutional treaty. There is some irony in the espousal of referenda by the Eurosceptics: the basic constitutional principle in Britain is the supremacy of parliament, with no procedural distinction between constitutional and other law. Referenda are more associated with continental countries, and then not always with their most democratic moments. The virus then spread to France and the Netherlands; in France in particular it was always going to difficult to resist calls for a popular vote on something calling itself a constitution, and Blair's decision in Britain made it impossible.

This was also the result of collective European hubris. For once the UK was right in arguing that this was not a constitution and should not be called one. Jack Straw's line that golf clubs also have constitutions was clever but it did not respond to the real point: golf clubs do not try to pretend that they are states—which was what the more ambitious members of the EU were about when they named the treaty a "constitution." One of the difficulties with the European Union is that even its friends do not well understand what it is—which is perhaps not surprising since it is still in the making. But this does not make it easy to explain, or a good subject for referenda. Its opponents on the other hand are all too certain they know what it is, and they do not want it (see Simon Berlaymont, "What the European Union is" (23 June 2005).

The balance-sheet

Blair's biggest European failure came also with a moment of hubris, primarily American. He too was also seduced by the glamour of power and the illusion of influence, just as his European colleagues were trapped by their desire to make the EU into something grander than it was. Iraq is the great failure of foreign policy under Blair; but it is also a failure of European policy.

At the heart of this failure is the unwillingness to take Europe seriously as a place to make foreign policy. The only way of standing up to America, of taking an independent line in classical foreign policy as well as in areas such as trade, is through the European Union. This requires a change of psychology on the part of Britain—which has never thought much about standing up to the US in the first place. A united European position on Iraq might have had a chance of persuading the US either not to invade until the case on weapons of mass destruction (WMD) had been proved (ie, as it turned out, never) or to have handled the campaign less incompetently. Perhaps not, of course. Perhaps there was no possibility at all of influencing the US in its hysterical, fearful, hubristic, mood at that time. What is certain is that Britain on its own had no influence; likewise France also on its own. And Europe divided had none either.

A joint policy by Britain and France might have had a chance of setting a different, more responsible and more influential, course for both countries and for Europe. The blame belongs in the Elysée [23] as well in Downing Street (both have implicitly recognised their failure by handling Iran in a strikingly different fashion). But the real failure is deeper.

Unless Europe is conceived of as the place where foreign policy is made (Peter Riddell in his excellent chapter in *The Blair Effect* [24] makes the point that the existence of separate advisers on foreign policy and European affairs in Downing Street tends to reinforce the idea that Europe is about technical matters and foreign policy takes place on a grander stage elsewhere); unless it is equipped with the machinery and the habits of mind and of action to cope with real crises—then it will always be easiest to revert to national escapism: grandstanding Gaullism in France, subservience to American power in Britain. Blair himself, with Chirac, began building that machinery at St Malo; the next stage (the creation of a jointly owned foreign service) was set in the constitutional treaty. This is slow and often tedious work but it remains the only way to a serious foreign policy.

As Geoff Mulgan [25] commented on leaving Downing Street, governments overestimate what they can change in the short term and underestimate what they can change in the long term. But the constant theme in Blair's speeches of Britain at the centre of a network of relationships, of which Europe is an important element but always mentioned co-equally with the United States, suggests that in the end the vision of a European alternative may never have been there in the first place.

Blair himself may see his greatest failure on Europe as the failure to create a pro-European public in Britain. In fact opinion polls suggest that opinion has become more anti-European during his term of office. To reverse this would be a Herculean task under the best of circumstances, given the difficulty of explaining the importance of Europe [26] to people who have lost their sense of history, and the distortions they are daily fed by the press. Perhaps this failure, crucial though it is, should not be taken too hard, since Britain is by no means unique in this respect. Such levelling down elsewhere may not be entirely undesirable if it means a more realistic view of what Europe is and what it can be; but it would be better if it were matched by some levelling up on the part of Britain.

Here the news is perhaps not uniformly bad. Away from the press and the opinion polls the visitor to Brussels today would be struck by the degree to which, in contrast to the 1980s and early 1990s, Britain operates as a normal European country, difficult at times—but then that is true of all the larger countries—but no longer automatically the awkward squad. In a world where lasting results are always achieved slowly, this may not be not such a bad record after all.

URLS

[1] europa.eu/abc/history/index_en.htm

[2] www.number-10.gov.uk/output/Page125.asp
[3] www.number-10.gov.uk/output/Page4.asp
[4] www.londonspeakerbureau.co.uk/speakers/viewSpeaker.aspx?speakerid=392
[5] www.historiasiglo20.org/europe/amsterdam.htm
[6] www.historiasiglo20.org/europe/niza.htm
[7] www.hm-treasury.gov.uk/about/ministerial_profiles/minprofile_brown.cfm
[8] www.euractiv.com/en/constitution/lisbon-agenda/article-117510
[9] www.spiegel.de/international/0,1518,379600,00.html
[10] www.tsoshop.co.uk/bookstore.asp?FO=1160642&DI=586620
[11] ec.europa.eu/agriculture/capreform/index_en.htm
[12] www.nato.int/issues/enlargement/index.html
[13] www.europarl.europa.eu/summits/hel1_en.htm
[14] www.gouvernement.lu/gouvernement/premier_ministre/cv_eng/index.html
[15] www.number-10.gov.uk/output/Page126.asp
[16] www.dti.gov.uk/energy/review/page31995.html
[17] news.bbc.co.uk/1/hi/uk_politics/227598.stm
[18] bakerinstitute.org/Per_Honorary_Chair.cfm
[19] www.cer.org.uk/articles/grant_prospect_oct03.html
[20] www.haaretz.com/hasen/pages/ShArt.jhtml?itemNo=862061&contrassID=1&
     subContrassID=1
[21] www.number-10.gov.uk/output/Page1769.asp
[22] www.polity.co.uk/book.asp?ref=9780745633312
[23] www.elysee.fr/elysee/elysee.fr/anglais/the_elysee_palace/history_of_the_
     elysee_palace/history_of_the_elysee_palace.20248.html
[24] www.cambridge.org/uk/politics/blair/toc.htm
[25] www.youngfoundation.org.uk/about/people/staff/geoff_mulgan
[26] www.prospect-magazine.co.uk/article_details.php?id=8214

Futures

From ethnicity to empathy: a new idea of Europe

Ash Amin
24 July 2003

> The dynamic intermingling of peoples in contemporary Europe is challenging definitions of the continent's identity based on ethnicity, indigeneity and myths of origin. This unstoppable and enriching diversity calls for a distinct new politics—one that reframes the very idea of Europe in terms of empathy with the stranger.

One question worth asking in the context of the current European Union Taking this as their departure point, the authors of *People Flow* [1] are right to invite fresh thinking on the kind of Europe we want to live in. Europe is now home to millions of people from non-European backgrounds, many religious and cultural dispositions, and networks of attachment based on diaspora connections and cultural influences from around the world.

Much of Europe has become multi-ethnic and multicultural in ways that are no longer reducible to its 'indigenous' ethno-cultural traditions. Europe is a site of longings rooted in myths of origin and tradition—regional, national and European—as well as a site of transnational and trans-European identities and attachments.

But the latter are no longer confined to so-called 'third country' people or cosmopolitans in the fast lane of global travel. They also affect most 'ordinary' people, routinely enmeshed in plural and global consumption norms and patterns, even if consciously averse to all things 'foreign'.

This paradox is masterfully captured by Iain Chambers [2] as he muses over what to make of the presence of a traditional Arab scribe who has set out a stall on the corner of a busy street in the centre of Paris:

> "Wearing sandals, a turban, wrapped in a *djellaba* against the autumnal chill, sitting opposite a brand new school, a multicoloured tubular-steeled piece of postmodern architecture, the immobile dignity of this public writer emphasises the disturbing presence of the stranger. His pen, his language, his being, is coeval with mine. I could turn away and pretend that he no longer exists; that he is merely a quaint remnant of yesterday's immigration from the 'Third World', from the Maghreb. I can choose to see in his presence merely the intrusion of the exotic and the archaic in the mundane of modernity..."

Ideas of the old Europe

What is it to be European in this context? What can such diversity weave around in the name of a shared or common identity—one that does not work with a hierarchy of worth based on ethnic or racial markers? The Idea of Europe that has stood for so long as a defining feature of the old continent—in opposition, at different times, to tribal 'barbarism', religious society, communist or communalist organisation, and American individualism—draws on four core values that are supposed to define Europe's contribution to modernity.

The first is a commitment to the rule of (Roman) law; the second is solidarity based on Christian charity and mutuality; the third is a commitment to the institutions of liberal democracy, rooted in the recognition of the rights and freedoms of the individual; and the fourth value is an appeal to community based on reason, and other Enlightenment universals that bind humans wherever they are in 'civilised' association.

After 11 September 2001 and all that it has led to it in terms of the many rushed and thoughtless associations claimed between Islam, rogue states and terrorism, many western liberals have consciously returned to these core values to propose them as a new world standard of cohesion and civilisation, against the excesses of Americanism and, above all, the 'terrors' of religious fundamentalism.

But an appeal to this old Idea of Europe is dangerous on two counts in the new Europe of multicultural and multiethnic belongings, despite its claim upon universals of civic and public culture stripped of ethnic or nationalistic moorings.

First, the murmur of a war of crusade between Islam and the secular west arising out of the debris of Bosnia, 9/11, Palestine, Afghanistan, and Iraq, is forging a Eurocentric imaginary of a world split [3] into two camps: a 'West' seen to be peace-loving and civilised because of its Enlightenment and Christian humanist values and an 'East' seen to be bellicose and infantile or irresponsible because of its religious zealotry and tribal behaviour.

The old Idea of Europe is once again lending its name to demarcate a space of progress and superiority against other worlds defined in ethno-religious terms. The consequence, wittingly or not, is that the Idea of Europe has become synonymous with white, Christian, reasoning Europeans. Because of this association, it will be seen as culturally exclusionary by the world majority that is judged to be infantile and irresponsible. Western liberal intellectuals are arrogant to believe in the superiority or universalism of the kind of thinking that underlies the Idea of Europe.

Second, as universalistic moral pretensions come to be challenged by other world views—from Islam to post-colonial ideologies and various new global social movements—the old Idea of Europe will prove to be increasingly vulnerable as a motif for unity in Europe. Who will it appeal to and who will care enough to be carried by it? What will it mean to cosmopolitans and everyday consumers riding the swell of global, made-up-as-you go, affiliations? How will it fire the imagination and loyalty of minority ethnic groups with loyalties split between host nation and imagined communities dispersed around the world and set in non-European histories?

Indeed, will it mean much to the growing number of everyday folk in majority communities, who, destabilised by the presence of strangers in their midst, as well as by the complexities of multiple assaults on their identities, yearn for the simplicity and security of local community and ethno-national belonging?

These yearnings for cultural difference and distinction within Europe itself—some territorial and others dispersed—make the old Idea of Europe a blunt instrument for unity in a Europe that paradoxically is both too big and too small for too many people as a commons.

Ideas for a new Europe

The lack of a unifying ideal will tear an increasingly multi-ethnic and multicultural Europe apart. But, given the above reservations, any new Idea of Europe will have to be de-ethnicised as well as universalised in ways that allow for difference and diversity both within and beyond Europe, with no hierarchy of worth implied. The starting point cannot be the *Europeanness* of Europe, for example, or the appeal to philosophical principles whose ethnic and cultural biases are never far from the surface.

I propose, instead, to locate the alternative Idea of Europe within a philosophical ethos that publicises *empathy and engagement with the stranger as the essence of what it is to be 'European'*. As it happens, this ethos draws deeply on the pre-Socratic and Socratic [4] tradition of defining freedom as the product of dialogue and engagement.

Two pillars of a non-racial Idea of Europe spring out of this interpretation of what it is to be free. The first is the principle of *hospitality*, which Julia Kristeva [5] links etymologically to the original Greek 'ethos', defined as the habit of regular stay or shelter. This is an inspiring motif of belonging in Europe, one that Derrida [6] too has appealed to recently, in arguing for a recovery of European cities as sites of refuge and hospitality for travellers and those in need of sanctuary.

In a Europe in which we all might be strangers one day as we come to be routinely on the move—whether virtually or physically—from one cultural space to another, the principle of refuge will serve the interests of more than just the minority currently needing protection from persecution and hardship in their country of origin.

If the Europe to come increasingly resembles 'an aterritorial space in which all residents of European states would be in a position of exodus', as Giorgio Agamben [7] speculates, the consequence will be that 'the status of "European" would mean the being-in-exodus of the citizen ... decidedly opposing itself to the concept of nation'. The ethos of hospitality, and the various rights and protections that accompany it, might have to become something more than its current status as a grudging obligation by states towards marginals such as refugees, immigrants and asylum-seekers.

The second pillar of a new Idea of Europe implied by the Socratic idea that we are not born free, but become free through engagement, is the principle of *mutuality* as the basis on which identities are formed. Freedom follows from engagement with, and publicity for, the stranger in and among us, not least because without the stranger constituted as 'Other', the self cannot be defined. But it is also the case that the stranger—whether we like it or not—works away at our certitude of the purity of self-identity. For the stranger always comes with the paradox of self-assuredness and loss of self-identity. Iain Chambers therefore, proposes a different way to look at the Arab scribe on the street corner of Paris:

"... But I can also register a trace, not merely of another world largely hidden from my eyes and understanding, but rather the trace of a language and history that seeks a response, and a responsibility, in mine. Apparently a foreigner, this, too, is clearly his city—certainly more than it is 'mine'. Forced to consider the composite realisation of modern space as it comes into being in this cosmopolitan place called Paris, I also register the alterity that is both integral to it and to the modernity I presume to possess.... Separate, yet indissolubly linked, his presence both interrupts and reconfigures my history, translating the closure of my 'identity' into an aperture in which I meet another who is in the world, yet irreducible to my will."

A politics of engagement

In a multi-ethnic and multicultural Europe, any failure to openly acknowledge the principle of mutuality and all that it represents in shaping identities as well as ensuring cultural change, will play into the hands of ethno-nationalists and xenophobes—abundant in number in both majority and minority communities—interested in perpetuating the fiction of pure, homeland, cultural identities and territorial boundaries in Europe.

Europe has a clear choice to make. It can deny the processes of cultural heterogeneity and hybridisation daily at work and allow ethnicity-based antagonisms to grow, aided by an overarching White Europeanist ideal of the good life. Alternatively, it can recognise the coming Europe of plural and hybrid cultures and affiliations and seek to develop an imaginary of becoming European through engagement with the stranger in ways that imply no threat to tradition and cultural autonomy. This requires a Europe stripped of ethnicised and racialised judgements concerning the worth of those who find themselves there as citizens and residents.

Moreover, our argument implies a completely different understanding of what it is to be political. A notion of freedom based on becoming rather than being (given to a prior cause) points towards a new politics of Europe. It moves on from a programmatic politics based on pre-given notions of where Europe's historic mission [8] for itself and for the world at large lies, towards a politics of making Europe through the democratic clash of a multicultural and multiethnic public which, through engagement, becomes European in ways that have yet to be defined.

In Deleuzian [9] terms, the latter can be described as a diagrammatic politics, in the sense that it makes visible and traces potentialities, immanent tendencies and inter-cultural negotiations at or below ground level. Thus, neither a 'major' politics of grand normative designs for Europe—multicultural or otherwise—to be delivered by the state machinery at national or European level: nor a 'minority' politics of recognition based on fictive ethnicities crying out to be rewarded.

What we need instead is a 'minor' politics modest enough to see that 'in some sense we are all potentially from a strange "nowhere" prior to "territorial" definitions', a 'people to come'.

The proposition of a minor politics for Europe is not as bizarre as it first sounds. Indeed, we already live to some degree in a time of minor politics, even if those caught up in it pretend certainty of motive, origin and destination. Hidden under the shadow of state politics and grand narratives exists the febrile activity of a vast network of complementary and conflicting institutions and movements also shaping the cultural map of Europe, and tapping deep into the cultural practices of different communities.

In the field of ethnic relations alone, this network includes the politics of national imaginaries of assimilation and integration, structures of opportunity, welfare and cultural autonomy, business, popular and media practices towards majorities and minorities, the clash of racist and anti-racist organisations, public rhetoric on nation, Europe and strangers [10], and everyday negotiations of race and ethnicity in the labour market, in public spaces, in schools, and in neighbourhoods. Such assemblages are *de facto* an arena of minor politics, pulling people in different directions of ethno-cultural practice and attitude dependent on the balance of power and formative influences in given spatial and social contexts.

People to come

What an Idea of Europe [11] based on the ethos of empathy with the stranger can do, is to inflect minor politics in the direction of fruitful cultural dialogue and exchange. There is nothing intrinsically progressive or regressive about minor politics as such. A new Idea of Europe alone, however, is not enough. Other actions, at different levels of Europe, are necessary for a politics of engagement in Europe.

One reform that seems vital at the level of Europe, is the upward harmonisation of citizenship rights, but now offered as rights of residence too, in order to ensure that long-standing residents without EU citizenship are protected by adequate social, economic and political rights.

A constitutionally protected Europe of the commons that offers to all in Europe a harmonised set of generous welfare protections, basic economic rights, and the right to political expression and protection, will help to buffer some of the politics of envy that currently exists between national communities, and between disadvantaged or socially-excluded groups, which fuels ethnic and cultural suspicion and intolerance.

The offer of universal rights of 'personhood' based on residence rather than citizenship alone, will facilitate the 'being-in-exodus' that Giorgio Agamben [12] anticipates. Underpinning this condition of existence with equal mobile rights will help to reduce knee-jerk vilifications of the stranger and the xenophobia that feeds on competition for scarce material resources. Both the European Charter on Fundamental Rights [13] and the Constitutional Convention [14] currently under debate could be re-imagined as the bedrock for a new politics of engagement based on mutuality and hospitality.

A politics of engagement, though, must also attend to the local everyday. The authors of *People Flow* choose as one of their core principles, the premise that, 'The immediate environments of neighbourhood and school should be the major focus for efforts to respond constructively to diversity'. It is indeed in sites of daily encounter, from schools and the workplace to associations and public spaces, that the direct experience of race and ethnicity is shaped and negotiated.

The riots [15] in Bradford, Oldham, and Burnley in northern England during the summer of 2001, together with ample evidence of local ethnographies of race negotiations elsewhere in Europe, confirm the powers of the local everyday in shaping the nature of encounters with, and attitudes towards, the stranger.

Racial and ethnic relations vary from neighbourhood to neighbourhood, shaped by the intersection of local and wider currents of cultural influence in any given site. A new politics of inter-culturalism cannot ignore these site influences, or the potential of local experiments in dealing with ethnic and racial suspicion and conflict, through prosaic negotiations of cultural difference.

Many are the experiments of cultural transgression and understanding that can be cited, from the use of legislative theatre to help confront latent prejudice, through to the use of communal gardens, urban art, and school exchanges to foster cross-ethnic projects based on real engagement in common ventures, and new experiments in urban planning that encourage cultural exchange in public spaces as well as multiculturalism in the public culture. Though remote from the common actions fashioned in Brussels or Strasbourg, these experiments of the everyday that have lasting effects, also have a role to play in an Idea of Europe committed to becomings [16] through engagement.

URLS

[1] www.opendemocracy.net/debates/debate-10-96.jsp
[2] www.semcoop.com/detail/041524756X
[3] www.alamut.com/subj/economics/misc/clash.html
[4] www.wikipedia.org/wiki/Socrates
[5] www.crescentmoon.org.uk/cresmokris
[6] www.semcoop.com/detail/0804734062
[7] www.semcoop.com/detail/0816630364
[8] www.hum.gu.se/arkiv/BANTU-L/current/msg00041.html
[9] pratt.edu/~arch543p/help/Deleuze.html
[10] www.semcoop.com/detail/0312281803
[11] www.hi.gymfag.dk/pb_asia.pdf
[12] www.egs.edu/faculty/agamben.html
[13] www.europarl.eu.int/charter/default_en.htm
[14] european-convention.eu.int/bienvenue.asp?lang=EN
[15] news.bbc.co.uk/2/hi/uk_news/1435958.stm
[16] www.guardian.co.uk/eu/story/0,7369,997745,00.html

Europe and beyond: struggles for recognition

Kalypso Nicolaïdis

21 February 2006

> The services directive and the Mohammed cartoon affair each
> demonstrate the need for a spirit of managed mutual recognition
> in Europe and beyond, argues Kalypso Nicolaïdis.

The European parliament has finally passed its amended version of the controversial services directive while thousands protested at its gates. British prime minister Tony Blair and European Commission president José Manuel Barroso, the greens and conservatives in the parliament, trade unions [1] and business associations had all started the year by declaring that the liberalisation of services markets would be the key European issue in 2006.

In the event, the version churned out by the European parliament frustrates the hopes of Europe's liberals as it waters down [2] or removes the most liberalising provisions—including the "country of origin" principle that would have allowed companies to apply their own countries' domestic laws when providing services in other European states. Yet they should consider it a necessary compromise, compatible with their own philosophy.

Perhaps there is something to be learned by contrasting this debate with the other great controversy of the day—the publication and circulation in Europe of cartoons depicting the Muslim prophet, Mohammed.

In both cases, passionate advocates see grand principles pitted against one another. Freedom of movement against respect for sacred social laws; freedom of speech against respect for sacred symbols; socialism vs neo-liberalism; the west vs the rest.

And yet in neither case can we accept the framing of the issue in such stark terms. The real opposition is between self-righteousness on all sides and the difficult search for justice in a globalised world groping for ways to manage our increasingly conspicuous—if not actually greater—cultural and economic differences.

At the heart of both controversies lies the same paradox. If those of us who live in prosperous western Europe (and in other areas of the privileged global north) want people from elsewhere to better integrate in our economies and our societies we need to recognise the validity of at least some of their habits and rules from home. Only in the name of an old-fashioned defence of sovereignty and the absolute match between territorial, legal and administrative jurisdiction can we reject the multifaceted demand for recognition.

If people in the original heartland of the European Union want the countries of east-central Europe which joined the EU in 2004 to catch up, they cannot ask their small businesses and citizens to adapt all over again to each member-state's rules—and this is in a European space which is supposed to be borderless. Similarly, we cannot simply ignore the civic responsibilities (in Tariq Ramadan's [3] words) that come with Europe's claim to primacy in the so-called dialogue of civilisation with the Muslim world within and beyond our borders. Most Muslims cannot be expected to buy our hard-earned fondness of blasphemy wholesale, here and now. Recognition, be it of regulations or identities, means internalising the interests and beliefs of others.

A community of others

But we must not forget two crucial corollaries to the demand for recognition: that in order to be sustainable, recognition must be *mutual* and it must be *managed over time*.

Managed mutual recognition [4] implies that acceptance of other people's norms can and must be reciprocal, conditional, progressive, partial, negotiated, dynamic and predicated on critical safeguards, including basic compatibility between the customs and laws of the countries or communities involved. As the Hegelian philosopher Alexandre Kojève [5] pointed out, recognition is predicated on mutual trust as well as the consensual bargaining over the limits of such trust at any given point.

Indeed, the European single market [6] has been predicated on this subtle approach for the last twenty years, both for goods and services, including through the recognition of diplomas. So is the compromise adopted by the European parliament. The amended text reaffirms that the basic social laws of the host country will apply to workers and excludes from application "services of general economic interest" (like transport, energy and postal services).

At the same time, the text contains a built-in dynamic for the expansion of recognition over time. It enables governments to enforce local rules pursuing social, environmental, health, security, and consumer-protection objectives, but only to the extent that these are "necessary" and "proportional" to the goals pursued. In other words, if countries of origin do their job, they will see their laws recognised to the extent that the European Court of Justice [7], the commission and other associated interests remain keen to enforce non-discrimination to the fullest. The sphere of mutual recognition will expand in tandem with the requisite level of convergence and tolerance between social systems.

> Also in **openDemocracy** on the "cartoon war" in Europe and the Muslim world:
> Neal Ascherson, "A carnival of stupidity" (February 2006)
> "Muslims and Europe: a cartoon confrontation" (February 2006)—a compendium of views from twenty writers
> Doug Ireland, "The right to caricature God... and his prophets" (February 2006)
> Tariq Modood, "The liberal dilemma: integration or vilification? " (February 2006)
> Ehsan Masood, "A post-Satanic journey" (February 2006)
> Sarah Lindon, "Words on images: the cartoon controversy" [10] (February 2006)
> Fred Halliday, "Blasphemy and power" (February 2006)
> S Sayyid, "Old Europe, New World" (February 2006)
> Sakia Sassen, "Free speech in the frontier-zone" (February 2006)
> Daphna Vardi, "Jews and cartoons: why the connection? " (February 2006)

Which brings us back to the cartoon clash. For Europeans to be truly reconciled with recognising the sensitivities of Muslims (European or not, inside [8] or outside Europe), mutuality will certainly help. Muslim societies do not have to become like European societies—although more freedom of speech in many of them would be welcome—but they must understand that many of us hold sacred the right to express disrespect for religion.

Moderates ought to argue on the fine points—such as whether limits to free speech are legal or moral questions or whether bans should be considered in cases of disrespect or only where incitement to violence is involved. But surely, the hope is that—with time, greater convergence, mutual knowledge and indeed healthy non-violent conflict—the scope for mutual recognition will expand here too.

This is the European vision, if there is one: living with our differences and seeking to harmonise if and only if such differences are illegitimate.

Recognition is a tough call on all sides of the political spectrum. The left fears social dumping when recognition means importing market rules; libertarians fear political dumping when recognition means importing curbs on free speech. Even if these fears can be exploited to demonise Polish plumbers [9] or Muslim migrants, they must be assuaged. Ultimately, however, they must also be transcended if we are to live in Europe and in the world as a community of others.

URLS

[1] www.etuc.org/a/1982
[2] www.contractoruk.com/news/002522.html
[3] www.opendemocracy.net/debates/article-5-57-2006.jsp
[4] papers.ssrn.com/sol3/papers.cfm?abstract_id=728383
[5] www.iep.utm.edu/k/kojeve.htm
[6] www.politics.co.uk/issues/european-single-market-$2108036.htm
[7] www.curia.eu.int/en/instit/presentationfr/index_cje.htm
[8] service.spiegel.de/cache/international/0,1518,k-6817,00.html
[9] www.radio.com.pl/polonia/article.asp?tId=23419
[10] www.opendemocracy.net/faith-terrorism/summary_3256.jsp

A commonwealth for Europe

John Palmer

11 October 2006

> How large can and should the European Union be? A renewed model which combines integration, openness, stability, and the defence of core democratic principles may offer the best answer, says John Palmer.

The government of Finland—which currently holds the rotating presidency [1] of the European Union—is making an all-out effort to ensure that negotiations with Turkey on its application to join the EU are not wrecked by disagreements over Cyprus. In their summit in Brussels on 14-15 December 2006 [2], EU heads of government must decide whether the talks can be kept on track or whether a major crisis in relations with Turkey is now unavoidable.

The question of Turkey's [3] future relationship with the European Union is strategically important, but there is an even bigger unanswered question hovering over the entire debate: what will be and what should be the limits to the geographical enlargement of the EU?

It is a question given new salience by the crisis [4] in relations between Russia and Georgia (whose government has made no secret [5] of its desire to join the union at some future date). It is raised too by the fact that two rivals in the southern Caucasus, Armenia and Azerbaijan (with whom Europe has increasingly important energy [6] links), harbour the same ambition.

The EU gave approval [7] on 26 September 2006 for Bulgaria [p. 120] and Romania [8] to join in January 2007. But what will soon be the twenty-seven member-state union is already negotiating possible membership not only with Turkey but also with Croatia [9]. Moreover, a promise in principle to consider their membership has also been given to Albania and other former Yugoslav republics—Macedonia, Bosnia,

Serbia [10], Montenegro and (once its independent status has been agreed) Kosovo.

Even this is not the end of the story. Ukraine and Moldova have already made clear that they are working towards eventual EU accession as a major policy priority. Belarus [11] has been told it cannot be even considered before its authoritarian regime has been replaced by democracy.

Thus, leaving aside for one moment the Turkish question, it is increasingly clear that EU leaders intend to halt further enlargement [12] - for the foreseeable future—once the countries of the western Balkans have joined (perhaps towards the end of the 2010s). For the coming years the European Union needs to get its own house in order [p. 115] before it is remotely capable of taking responsibility for ever more members.

As well as continuing economic reform, the EU faces a major negotiation to fix its long-term future budget for the next decade and beyond. Above all, it must finally agree on how to streamline, strengthen and democratise its own decision-making institutions. The hope is that by the end of 2008 agreement will finally be reached on a new treaty [13] (which, I suspect, will look rather similar to the one already approved by fifteen member-states but which was rejected by France [14] and the Netherlands [p. 94] in May-June 2005).

A third way

Assuming all of this falls into place—a new treaty by 2008, a new budget deal by 2010, and the beginning of the final stage of "classical" enlargement with the western Balkans and Turkey [15] —what then? There appear to be two, equally problematic, options. The first is that classical enlargement continues until it reaches Vladivostok (or beyond). This is difficult to see. Even with radical reform, the EU could not be expected to integrate so many peoples [16], leaping over so many time-zones and with such diverse national environments.

The second option is to choose "friendship," "cooperation," "neighbourhood relations" and other apple-pie links with the European Union's neighbours to the east. But what does that mean in practice? Very little. Aspirant EU member-countries in eastern Europe, the Caucasus [17] and beyond know that without actual "membership" they would have almost no real leverage, if any at all, over their European partners.

Until now it has been assumed that anything a European country joins should be the EU as it is. But there might be a different way of looking at all of this. The third possibility is something I would describe as a European Commonwealth [18]. It would have some similarities with the EU, but would demand less in terms of shared sovereignty and the scale of common policies. This would require beginning to think about some limited forms of sovereignty-sharing and collective institutions that might unite an enlarged European Union with wider neighbours, maybe in two configurations: one involving countries to the east, and the other with Mediterranean neighbours whose circumstances are very different.

At present the response of EU leaders (both in Brussels and the member-states) is: "We can't do this. We have to deal bilaterally with each country separately and limit relations to cooperation agreements." But countries like Ukraine [19], Georgia and others will only accept these as a staging-post to eventual membership. They want eventual joint decision-making and a voice in a larger common European body so that they are not merely on the receiving end of decisions taken by the EU alone, but partners in a shared enterprise.

If such a commonwealth comes into being it is an open question whether Turkey might prefer that to joining the EU itself. That decision can only be taken sometime after 2015 when Turkey is ready and the EU as a whole too is ready for a much more ambitious relationship. For now the priority must be to keep the Turkish path [20] to EU accession open. That is vital for continuing economic and political reform—above all for establishing a human-rights proof legal system in which the military are unambiguously under democratic civilian control.

A future European Commonwealth might have a limited mandate based on shared sovereignty and common law. But this could embrace important policy areas. After all, the current EU-Russia cooperation agreement [21] signed in 2005 envisages—in theory—a common space for trade and economic development, a common area of security, a common system of "legal principles," and a common area for research and development. This would exclude other essential features of EU integration such as a common currency, a common internal market, and social and environmental policies.

URLS

[1] www.eu2006.fi/the_presidency/en_GB/finland_as_a_host/
[2] www.eu2006.fi/calendar/vko50/en_GB/1136456998803/?calYear=2006&calMonth=11
[3] www.euractiv.com/en/enlargement/eu-turkey-negotiations/article-145219
[4] www.opendemocracy.net/democracy-caucasus/georgia_russia_3972.jsp
[5] www.mfa.gov.ge/index.php?sec_id=125&lang_id=ENG
[6] www.rferl.org/featuresarticle/2006/06/ec9c0bef-10c7-43b4-8bad-f9612fc6317e.html
[7] www.iht.com/articles/2006/09/26/news/union.php
[8] www.opendemocracy.net/democracy-europefuture/EU_romania_3943.jsp
[9] www.euractiv.com/en/enlargement/eu-croatia-relations/article-129605
[10] mondediplo.com/2006/10/09serbia
[11] www.opendemocracy.net/globalization-institutions_government/denim_3441.jsp
[12] europa.eu/scadplus/glossary/enlargement_en.htm
[13] europa.eu/scadplus/glossary/constitution_en.htm
[14] www.opendemocracy.net/democracy-europe_constitution/democractic_deficit_3610.jsp
[15] www.opendemocracy.net/democracy-europefuture/membership_2896.jsp
[16] www.opendemocracy.net/democracy-europefuture/article_1647.jsp
[17] www.iwpr.net/index.php?apc_state=henpcrs&s=o&o=caucasus_map.html
[18] www.policy.lv/index.php?id=103145&lang=en
[19] www.opendemocracy.net/democracy-ukraine/issue.jsp
[20] www.opendemocracy.net/democracy-turkey/debate.jsp
[21] www.euractiv.com/en/enlargement/eu-russia-sign-deal-bid-disputes/article-139268

The European Union at fifty: a second life

Aurore Wanlin

15 March 2007

The European Union's half-century is a time for constructive self-reflection as much as celebration, says Aurore Wanlin.

On 25 March 2007, the European Union will celebrate the fiftieth anniversary of the treaty of Rome, the founding document of what became today's union of twenty-seven member-states. The occasion will be marked by a summit conference of leaders in Berlin (whose German hosts currently hold the rotating presidency [1]) on 24-25 March [2], from where a major "Berlin declaration" will be proclaimed. The document is expected to contain a resounding statement of the European Union's values and principles as it looks forward to the next fifty years.

This is all quite appropriate as far as it goes: landmark birthdays are occasions for a certain ceremony and rhetorical extravagance. Equally, however, the cost of overdoing things can be painful. Perhaps the most satisfying such events are those where justified pride [3] at having passed an existential milestone is combined with calm awareness of the path that has led to this point. Such introspection is difficult in the midst of fixed patterns of thinking, routines and relationships built up over a long period. But it is essential if healthy life and development are to be sustained.

This, then, is the test for the European Union leaders in Berlin. The challenge they face is threefold: to come to a balanced assessment of the successes and failures of the EU's fifty-year journey, to honestly examine what works and what doesn't in the present-day union, and to look ahead with a clear understanding that the issues the union will face in the next half-century will be very different from those in the last. If they manage all of that, they will deserve their champagne [4].

The history of the present

In many ways, the European Union has been a success. A club of six countries has grown into a far-reaching political organisation with twenty-seven member-states and 500 million inhabitants, which represents the world's biggest economic and trading bloc. It has been a facilitator and guarantor of peace, stability and prosperity to most of a continent that in the decades before its creation had been ravaged by national strife and international wars.

In institutional terms, it has survived countless internal splits, angry summits, "empty chairs" and years of "eurosclerosis"—while continuing to attract more aspirants to membership and to incorporate them efficiently in a gradual process of enlargement. The ability of the European Union to sustain its core identity and architecture while being open to continual change is surely one index of fundamental health.

At the same time, it cannot be denied that the EU today is at a crossroads. The French and Dutch people's rejection of the EU draft constitution in the referenda of May-June 2005 brought the constitutional development of the union to a shuddering standstill from which it has yet to recover. Several of the union's defining policies—such as the common currency (the euro [5]) and the common agricultural policy (CAP)—are excoriated by critics but have diminishing support even among many former advocates. Politicians doubt the EU's relevance in a global economy and whether it is still capable of making Europe stronger and more competitive. Perhaps even more seriously for a project whose ultimate lifeblood is democratic legitimacy, many voters across the EU seem to have lost faith in the European Union as in any vital sense "theirs" to own. In an age when most people no longer fret over the risk of another "European civil war" [6], the prevailing view of Europe is less governed by its constructive role in the decades after 1945 [7] and more by the image of a remote, bureaucratic and in some ways undemocratic organisation.

The contrast between the EU's past achievements and today's inertia, then, can appear striking. But the surrender to a nostalgia which sees much of the last fifty years as a golden age would be no solution.

A clear illustration is the tendency to contrast the great pioneers of European unity—men such as Jean Monnet [8], Robert Schuman [9] or Paul-Henri Spaak [10] —with their far more anonymous (and in many cases indifferent in performance) successors. It is true that Europe has been relatively unfortunate over recent years with its heads of state and governments: most have been short of pro-European feelings and have proved all too keen to defend short-term national interests at the expense of a long-term vision for Europe.

However, exceptional people often spring from exceptional circumstances. Jean Monnet [11], Robert Schuman or Paul-Henri Spaak and their contemporaries were arguably able to achieve so much because their moral qualities and ideas had been tested and developed by living through the horrors of the second world war; without the latter, they might never have come to power at all. Today's European Union leaders may not be extraordinary, but individual leaders with grand visions rarely thrive easily in peaceful and prosperous societies. They must meet the challenge of their own and not yesterday's times.

A look in the mirror

There is still much to learn from the European Union's inheritance [12]. The lessons are there if the past is interrogated in a questioning and constructive spirit, and treated as resource and inspiration rather than monument. The forthcoming anniversary celebration offers a valuable opportunity for deliberation and discussion that in looking back also clears the way to modern, fresh, outward-looking [13] thinking. Here, then are six lessons from an assessment of the EU's fifty-year experience:

Do not ask the EU to do what it cannot do. National leaders should give up grand ambitions and grandiose rhetoric that cannot be sustained in practice. The mismatch between the Lisbon agenda's [14] original ambition of turning the EU into "the most competitive knowledge-based economy" and the actual outcome is a perfect illustration. The national governments' failure to meet their targets may have discredited [15] the agenda itself and reinforced European citizens' scepticism about the EU's ability to deliver: a devastating double-blow. It is true that the EU as a whole cannot be expected the burden of responsibility, as the Lisbon agenda's implementation depends mainly on the member-states; but the French and Dutch "no" vote on the draft constitution [16] demonstrated that citizens hold the EU as well as their own governments to account for the comparative lack of growth and jobs in Europe

Give the union the means to fulfil its objectives. National governments have become increasingly wary about surrendering levers of power and authority to the union in order for it to advance the goals to which all are formally committed. Energy policy is a good example of an area that everybody agrees is crucial to Europe's future, and one where most agree that integrated action at the EU level would have clear benefits. Yet EU leaders do not seem prepared either to make the necessary compromises to create a truly level playing-field over energy production and distribution, or to define a common position towards Europe's crucial interlocutor in this field, namely Russia.

Clarify the division of labour between the EU and national member-states. Citizens are asking for, even demanding, more clarity. To achieve it was part of the objective of the draft constitution, but its efforts can in retrospect be seen as too timid. In the next stage, some policies may indeed need to be "repatriated" to the national level. At the same time, any such reform must be thoroughly discussed and very carefully implemented; to unpick the *acquis communautaire* [17] (the body of shared regulations that must be incorporated into a member-state's national legislation as a condition of accession) could also lead to an unravelling of the union. EU leaders should ensure that they do not empty the union of any substance, and indeed—in looking forward to the major defining issues of the next decades, such as climate change [18] —they should not fear transferring new competences to the EU. Gordon Brown, Britain's prime-minister-in-waiting, is among those politicians (by no means all on the narrowly "Eurosceptic" right or left) who question whether the EU is still relevant in a global economy. The debate is important. But some answers are already obvious: energy, migration, scientific research [19], as well as global warming are all areas where union-wide cooperation is vital and where the EU can clearly add value. But it can only do this if it has the necessary competences and the financial means to act accordingly

Match the EU's budget to its delivery, and both to the institutional debate. The review of the union's budget offers a unique opportunity to put money where the mouths of most EU leaders are. It will provide national governments with the opportunity to clarify the overall situation and take responsibility for areas of cooperation among different member-states that want to act together and deliver. The EU's overall budget may be too small, but it would be wrong to decide to increase it simply for the sake of meeting the presumed needs of an enlarged EU. Rather, it should be carefully prepared and linked to the institutional debate. French voters rejected the constitution in part because it failed to answer the question: "what is the EU for?" If the EU leaders link these two issues, they would gain a triple benefit: create space to try to answer that question afresh and in practical terms, give the EU a new sense of direction [20], and—most importantly—provide it with the means to deliver

Also in **openDemocracy** on the European Union's past, present and future:
Simon Berlaymont, What the European Union is [p. 81] (23 June 2005)
Krzysztof Bobinski, Democracy in the European Union, more or less [22] (27 July 2005)
Kalypso Nicolaïdis, Europe and beyond: struggles for recognition [p. 159] (21 February 2006)
Frank Vibert, 'Absorption capacity': the wrong European debate [p. 108] (21 June 2006)
Anthony Barnett, The birth of Europe? [23] (9 October 2006)
John Palmer, Germany and Europe: the pull of unity [24] (16 February 2007)

Maintain the community method of decision-making. The traditional community method is by far the best the EU has had so far. Would the commission have launched and realised the single market using the "open method of coordination?" The EU is strong if its institutions—the commission [21] in particular—are strong. An honest broker capable of defining common ground that satisfies all governments despite their widely diverging starting-points is essential to achieving its goals. True, the single market probably needs to be reviewed; the EU economy has changed since it was launched in the 1980s. But the role of the commission, and the community method at the core of its operations, should remain central

Style matters. EU governments cannot expect the EU to work if a leader criticises others for being badly brought up, if ministers never show up to council meetings, and if most blame the EU for decisions they themselves took. Some politicians do not hesitate to make unrealistic and protectionist promises to their national electorates at general-election time. But all should remember that the union in itself has been one of the most unique and extraordinary achievements of Europe over the last century. It is a fragile and vulnerable heritage, however. It needs to be improved, but mostly because it is and has always been a work in progress. That may be even truer now, when the world is changing so quickly. But preserving it is also the responsibility of all its leaders.

A seventh lesson at the end, then: leadership, too, still matters. Let's hope the summiteers in Berlin are listening.

URLS

[1] www.eu2007.de/en/The_Council_Presidency/What_is_the_Presidency/index.html
[2] www.eu2007.de/en/Meetings_Calendar/Dates/March/0324-RAA.html
[3] europa.eu/50/index_en.htm
[4] www.eu2007.de/en/News/Press_Releases/March/0313BPAFest.html
[5] ec.europa.eu/economy_finance/euro/our_currency_en.htm
[6] www.panmacmillan.com/Titles/displayPage.asp?PageTitle=Individual%20Title&BookID=369237&International
[7] us.penguingroup.com/nf/Book/BookDisplay/0,,0_9781594200656,00.html
[8] www.historiasiglo20.org/pioneers/monnet.htm
[9] www.historiasiglo20.org/pioneers/schuman.htm
[10] www.historiasiglo20.org/pioneers/spaak.htm
[11] www.jean-monnet.ch/en/pMonnet/monnet5.php
[12] europa.eu/scadplus/glossary/eu_communities_en.htm
[13] ec.europa.eu/comm/external_relations/human_rights/intro/index.htm#1
[14] europa.eu/scadplus/glossary/lisbon_strategy_en.htm
[15] centreforeuropeanreform.blogspot.com/2007/03/what-is-wrong-with-lisbon-by-aurore.html
[16] europa.eu/scadplus/glossary/constitution_en.htm
[17] en.euabc.com/word/12
[18] europa.eu/50/news/theme/070209_kyoto_en.htm
[19] europa.eu/scadplus/leg/en/s23000.htm
[20] www.eu2007.de/en/The_Council_Presidency/trio/index.html
[21] europa.eu/scadplus/glossary/european_commission_en.htm
[22] www.opendemocracy.net/democracy-europe_constitution/yes_2704.jsp
[23] www.opendemocracy.net/democracy-europe_constitution/european_citizens_3975.jsp
[24] www.opendemocracy.net/democracy-europe_constitution/germany_4356.jsp

The European Union in 2057

Frank Vibert
22 March 2007

Its first half-century has been a qualified success for the European Union. Its fate in the next depends on its ability to look outward, says Frank Vibert.

On 1 July 1942, two weeks before the French authorities sent her to die in Auschwitz, Irène Némirovsky [1] confided in her notebook that the future offered only a choice between "two socialisms:" national socialism and communism. Fortunately, she was wrong. Today, both types of socialism are dead and the countries of Europe are part of a club of market-oriented democracies that form the European Union—a future that the novelist [2], and most of her European contemporaries, could not have envisaged.

Against this history, the European Union that celebrates in Berlin on 24-25 March 2007 [3] the fiftieth anniversary of the signing of the Treaty of Rome, can be seen as an enormous and historically unprecedented success. Yet the celebrations [4] are muted, staged and artificial. The reason for this seems to be that while the union can look back with pride it does not look forward with confidence. Few of its members wish to leave but few regard it with affection.

Grand themes vs everyday lives

In order to reverse a widespread sense of malaise within the union, Europe's intellectual or political leaders proffer various unifying themes. A constitution has been tried and failed. Further enlargement of the union's membership would extend what is arguably its greatest triumph, but is up against popular resistance. World leadership in the fight against environmental disaster has been proclaimed [5]. But the reality is that the member-states do not have energy policies consistent with their carbon-reduction targets. Some view a more credible common defence and security policy as a goal—but no government is spending the sums that would earn credibility. Leadership in the fight against global poverty is seen as more attractive by others—but the record of European interventions in sub-Saharan Africa does not inspire confidence.

Different voices suggest that the whole idea of searching for grand unifying themes is a mistake. According to these voices what is required is for the union to demonstrate policies that work to benefit people in their everyday life, enhance job security and protect against social change. The existing institutions [6] should be allowed to get on with their jobs, as they are, without further navel-gazing. Those policies that do not work at a union level should be restored to the national and local level so that people do not feel so disconnected from remote and bureaucratic processes in Brussels. "Policy relevance" [7] is the catchphrase.

Fifty years ahead

In 2057, when people come to celebrate the union's centenary [8], they may look at this cacophony with bemusement. With hindsight it is always possible to spot trends and processes that were not so obvious at the time. What might these be?

A first important development might be the emergence of London in the first decade of the 21st century as Europe's pre-eminent and indeed only global centre [9] - a centre based on competitive and worldwide services: in finance, law, accounting, medicine, communications, entertainment and higher education. For London, Europe is only part of its market and not the most dynamic part. London is cosmopolitan while it is continental Europe rather than Britain that is insular. London offers opportunities for the young while an ageing Europe tries to protect those who already have jobs. Is London the market-led model of success the example that the union decided to foster and emulate in its second fifty years? Did Europe become a continent of newly great cities [10] rather than once great nation-states, a private-service economy rather than a state-service economy?

A second pivotal development to be identified in retrospect might be that obscure € 140 million ($187 million) item included for the first time in the European Union's 2007 budget under the category of the European Instrument for Democracy and Human Rights (EIDHR [11]). Did the union come to realise that, confronted with an inevitable decline in its own relative economic weight in the world economy, it would make a huge difference to its future comfort and security if the new powers in the world were going to be democratic or not?

Europe had seen the rise of greater powers outside its borders in the past—the United States and the Soviet Union. It was not their economic and military rise that mattered but the values they stood for. One offered hope for Europe and the other destruction. Faced with the rise of yet new powers, did the union therefore start linking more clearly its own "soft power" in trade and aid and its "hard power" in force-projection to democratisation outside its borders? Did the launching by Angela Merkel [12] in 2007 of a new effort to form a transatlantic partnership mark the end of sniping at the United States by Europe's politicians and intellectuals and a realisation that the union and America had to stand together in order to uphold democratic values in the world?

A third major development that future historians might identify could be the changes that took place in the organisation of democratic systems of government around the end of the 20th century and the beginning of the 21st. There was a turn towards relying on unelected bodies for problem-solving in democratic societies. They were better at marshalling the evidence and knowledge than elected politicians. Citizens wanted to be better informed about matters that affected their daily lives and found that unelected bodies were more likely to get out the information and to tell the truth than elected politicians. Indepen-

Also in **openDemocracy** on the European Union's past, present and future: Kalypso Nicolaïdis, We the peoples of Europe... [16] (18 December 2003) Simon Berlaymont, What the European Union is [p. 81] (23 June 2005) Anthony Barnett, The birth of Europe? [17] (9 October 2006) John Palmer, Germany and Europe: the pull of unity [18] (16 February 2007) Aurore Wanlin, The European Union at fifty: a second life [p. 167] (15 March 2007) Krzysztof Bobinski, European unity: reality and myth [p. 76] (21 March 2007)

dent unelected bodies came to be seen as a new branch of democratic systems of government, as important for the health of democratic societies in their way as an independent judiciary in its way. Informed citizens remained active democrats but they did not like the kind of sterile political debates they were offered or the old-fashioned parties they could choose from. Eventually this new separation of powers helped the union to sort out its own form of governance (for a discussion of the new separation of powers in relation to the union's existing power-sharing arrangements, see *The Rise of the Unelected*, Cambridge University Press, May 2007 [13]).

The challenge of uncertainty

The fact that there is so much uncertainty about the direction the European Union should take, and so much questioning of its form and structure, is not necessarily a sign of weakness. The union has proved itself [14] an effective bargaining forum for its members and an effective way of reconciling differences of viewpoint between them. This internal orientation has now to be replaced by an equally effective external orientation [15]. In this respect the example of the City of London is double edged. It shows how successful and vibrant a market-led Europe could be. But it also shows that the union could become damaging and irrelevant if it does not relate successfully to the larger world.

URLS

[1] www.randomhouse.com/author/results.pperl?authorid=62300
[2] www.randomhouse.com/knopf/catalog/display.pperl?isbn=9781400096275
[3] www.eu2007.de/en/Meetings_Calendar/Dates/March/0324-RAA.html
[4] europa.eu/50/index_en.htm
[5] www.timesonline.co.uk/tol/news/world/europe/article1492647.ece
[6] www.evropa.bg/en/del/europe-a-to-z/eu-institutions.html
[7] www.routledge.com/textbooks/0415358140/about/default.asp
[8] eubookshop.com/1/187
[9] www.pwc.com/extweb/ncpressrelease.nsf/docid/1C917B3A01FAE5558525729600708154
[10] giussani.typepad.com/loip/2006/09/global_federali.html
[11] www.welcomeurope.com/default.asp?id=1110&idpgm=11816
[12] www.bundeskanzlerin.de/nn_127722/Content/EN/Reden/2007/02/2007-02-10-rede-merkel-m_C3_BCnchner-sicherheitskonferenz.html
[13] www.cambridge.org/uk/catalogue/catalogue.asp?isbn=0521694140
[14] www.bundesregierung.de/nn_6538/Content/EN/Artikel/2007/03/2007-03-19-bkin-merkel-in-rom__en.html

[15] forsvar.regeringen.se/sb/d/7417/a/78898
[16] www.opendemocracy.net/democracy-think_tank/article_1647.jsp
[17] www.opendemocracy.net/democracy-europe_constitution/european_citizens_3975.jsp
[18] www.opendemocracy.net/democracy-europe_constitution/germany_4356.jsp

European Union: from backdoor to front

Michael Bruter

3 July 2007

The European Union's political progress starts with myth-clearing and continues with a democracy-making that builds on its citizens' sense of European identity, says Michael Bruter.

In the small hours of 23 June 2007, the twenty-seven heads of states and governments of the European Union reached an agreement at their summit [1] in Brussels on the amending treaty to replace the proposed EU constitution that French and Dutch voters rejected by referendum in 2005. The response among large segments of the press in Britain in particular was familiar; as on every occasion when a proposed new treaty is signed, they pointed an accusatory finger at the leaders responsible (in this case, departing British prime minister Tony Blair and his successor Gordon Brown) for betraying Britain and its national interest.

The opposition Conservative Party—equally predictably—joined the chorus, accusing these leaders of the equivalent of high treason and demanding an immediate referendum. To this, Blair and Brown on the centre-left as well as Kenneth Clarke on the centre-right explained that this was only an amending treaty, which changed the functioning of EU institutions far less than Maastricht [2] (1992), Amsterdam [3] (1997) or Nice [4] (2000); and that, moreover, it respected the four "red lines" announced by the outgoing and incoming prime ministers. They really made it sound like a small technical agreement which it is better not to talk about too much.

This claim that everything about the European Union is really technical rather than political (think of the so called "five tests" designed by Gordon Brown to decide whether or not Britain should join the eurozone) is systematically perceived by a majority of voters as a "backdoor" strategy. It is the equivalent of someone with absolutely nothing wrong in their luggage blushing and acting nervously when walking past customs officers at the airport. However unfairly, it cannot fail to arouse suspicion.

A majority of voters will thus believe that the agreement [5] reached at the Brussels meeting probably *must be* bad indeed, even though political experts across the ideological range privately agree that it actually makes Britain better off in a number of ways and worse off in none. Considering that Tony Blair, Gordon Brown, and Kenneth Clarke are some of the shrewdest and most intelligent politicians in the country, why on earth would they choose such an apparently dumb "backdoor" tactic, one that will always make them look suspicious in the eyes of the public?

The answer is probably threefold. First, they think that the people, however suspicious, will not be worried enough to actually *do* anything (this is a variation of what political scientists call the "permissive consensus." Second, they believe that—largely because of a fiercely Eurosceptic [6] press and the negative prejudices accumulated by public opinion for years—a "front-door" policy would be destined to fail, however good the treaty might be. Third, pro-Europeans like Blair and Clarke probably hope that ultimately, Europe will impose itself, because they believe it is a good thing for the country and that it will "grow into" the British people and find acceptance among them.

Their reasoning is as understandable as that of those citizens who believe that if the government tries to sneak Europe through the backdoor, there must be a catch. However, both positions are most probably equally mistaken. It is clearly for every individual citizen to decide how he or she stands with regards to European integration; but at the very least, it is time to correct a few myths about the new treaty, about Europe in general, and about public opinion and European identity in Britain. Here, then, are ten of the many such myths, recycled in various forms of media and public discourse in the aftermath of the Brussels summit.

Ten myths about Europe

Myth 1: "There is a catch"

When someone blushes on the way past the customs people, it usually signals fear of what they might be thinking rather than shame for what the person is carrying. The British government's defensiveness and low profile about the amending treaty derives not from any shame about its contents but from the immense power of a Eurosceptic media that focuses all its energies and narratives on reinforcing anti-EU prejudice. This makes it difficult if not impossible for a fundamentally pro-European leader to find level ground on which to support the argument for Europe; and base political calculation can make cowardice a more attractive short-term option.

Myth 2: "It is not what we signed for"

Yes it is. Individuals are entitled to think that signing was or was not a good idea, but the suggestion that the United Kingdom was (in 1973) joining a European Economic Community [7] that was or would remain "only" a free-market area is indefensible historically and absurd in principle. The Rome treaty of 1957 [8] was a monument of federalist prose, much more so than any subsequent European Union agreement. It made extremely ambitious declarations about citizenship, a common foreign policy, and more; its flaw was that it did not do a good job at setting out the rules to achieve them. In fact, the Paris treaty of 1951 [9] had been even more federalist, and it was also part of the package Britain ratified in 1973. People can sign documents without reading them, but the fact cannot be denied that Britain signed up to a political Europe [10] with both hands and with eyes wide open.

Myth 3: "The new treaty creates EU embassies for the first time"

No it doesn't. These embassies already exist and have existed for over fifty years! The first delegations of the European commission [11] were created in the 1950s, have expanded ever since, and became delegations of the European Union with the Amsterdam treaty. According to diplomatic protocol, the heads of delegations since the 1960s must be referred to as "ambassadors," and the delegations are on the list of state representations, not international organisations (as well as arguably doing a very good job in helping European citizens and companies).

What the treaty does in this area is to remove these delegations from the monopolistic control of the European commission ("Brussels") and transfer control to the new foreign-policy representative, who will be chosen by the member-states. It also adds professional diplomats from national civil services to the commission civil servants who have hitherto staffed them.

Myth 4: "European institutions are less trustworthy then national ones"

Well, in any case, they are more trusted. In 1980 there was no country in Europe where the European commission was more trusted than the national government or where the European parliament was more trusted than the national one. In 2004, people in fourteen of the fifteen member-states trusted [12] the European commission more than their national government, and thirteen of the fifteen trusted the European parliament more than the national one. And in both cases, the British people trusted the European institution more than the national one.

Myth 5: "Thank goodness we have opt-outs!"

Today, citizens from twenty-six of the EU's member-states are protected against such things as the government retaining their DNA samples if they have committed no offence, or the said government selling the DNA in question to private companies. The European Court of Justice [13] will in each case defend the rights of citizens if these are violated. But none of this applies to Britain, whose people will not benefit from the same protection. Is that so wonderful? The problem with opt-outs [14] is that they are usually symbolic ways for a state to show its difference; however, they always apply to rights, never to duties. That is why choosing to opt out is worse than taking the whole package 99% of the time.

Myth 6: "The European union is a massive bureaucracy"

There are fewer civil servants [15] working for the whole of the EU administration and its 490 million inhabitants than in the city of Cardiff alone!

Also in **openDemocracy** on the European Union's Brussels summit:
John Palmer, "Europe: the square root of no" (20 June 2007)
Kalypso Nikolaïdis & Philippe Herzog, "Europe at fifty: a new single act" (21 June 2007)
John Palmer, "Europe's next steps" (26 June 2007)
Krzysztof Bobinski, "The Polish confusion" (28 June 2007)

Myth 7: "Tony Blair surrendered the national veto in forty major policy areas"

Almost none of the areas where the June 2007 agreement [16] replaced unanimity by majority-vote is in any way significant. Moreover, in many of these cases it was none other than the United Kingdom that had persistently asked for majority rule, sometimes since the Margaret Thatcher [17] years! For example, in the context of immigration policy, most EU member-states support the tough British view—but one or two "softer" countries have so far been blocking the imposition of stricter regulation and control, and majority rule is seen as a way of overcoming this.

Thus, it is mistaken in the extreme to think that the UK is always the reluctant, lagging element in Europe and never in a proactive, demanding position. Rather, London is always seeking more integration or simplification in a number of areas; though of course, it cannot impose on others the choice of where to go further and where not. By and large, in the Tony Blair years, Britain has been highly successful at pushing its agenda.

Myth 8: "Europe costs us more than it brings us"

The problem in cost-benefit evaluations, as any political scientist knows, is that it is always much easier to put a clear figure on costs than to evaluate benefits. The positive outcomes of (for example) major transport projects or medical research are almost always less immediately visible and calculable than the expense they entail. In the case of the European Union, Britain's net contribution (in pure tax terms) is extremely small, after taking into account the large sums of money paid by the EU to help regional regeneration and public infrastructures like new roads and railways, as well as the rebate. The indirect financial gains (as evaluated by financial institutions and British companies) are arguably enormous. There are also many non-financial benefits which enrich people's lives and which they seem to enjoy even more.

Myth 9: "British people feel less and less European"

In surveying time-series data between 1973 and 2005, I found [18] that the average index score of declared European identity among British people has been multiplied by 2.5. True, levels of European identity in Britain remain lower than in most (not all) EU memberstates, but their increase has been more rapid than in the majority of its neighbours.

Also in **openDemocracy** on the European Union in a decisive year:
Aurore Wanlin, "The European Union at fifty: a second life" (15 March 2007)
Krzysztof Bobinski, "European unity: reality and myth" (21 March 2007)
Frank Vibert, "The European Union in 2057" (22 March 2057)
George Schöpflin, "The European Union's troubled birthday" (23 March 2007)
Mats Engström, "Europe's green power" (26 March 2007)
Simon Berlaymont, "Tony Blair and Europe" (30 May 2007)

Here, I distinguish between two components of European identity [19], civic and cultural, and find that whilst most Europeans feel in the main "civically" European, British and Swedish citizens feel predominantly "culturally" European. This makes perfect sense: when asked what it means to them to be European, most citizens refer to freedom of movement and borderlessness (embodied in the Schengen agreements), and then to the euro [20]. The United Kingdom has stayed out of both projects, which means that it simply does not mean the same thing to be a European Union citizen in the UK as it does in (for example) Germany, Finland, or France.

In every single member-state, levels of European identity rose sharply after the implementation of the Schengen agreement [21] and the circulation of the euro (but there was no evidence of such a surge preceding these initiatives). Arguably, a lack of courage among British politicians in arguing for the euro and Schengen has prevented citizens from being in a position to choose to experience what other citizens claim is the best part of the EU.

Myth 10: "We can't agree with anyone else on Europe"

All surveys show that citizens of all member-states—from Britain to Spain, from Denmark to France, from Ireland to Hungary—agree that the EU should be made more democratic. All citizens want significantly more powers to be transferred to the European parliament, and a vast majority want to be able to directly elect a president of the European Union rather than have him or her appointed for them. The heads of states and governments refuse these reforms (short of some marginal extensions of the co-decision procedure which gives more power to the European parliament) because the obscurity of decision-making procedures offers them political protection when they want to use the European Union to take the lead on some necessary but unpopular measures.

The conclusion is as compelling as it is self-evident. The way forward in Europe, which is also the only one majorities in all member-states (including Britain) support, is to pursue a process which most politicians do not yet have the courage to endorse: daring to make the European Union more democratic.

URLS

[1] www.eu2007.de/en/Meetings_Calendar/Dates/June/0621-ER.html
[2] europa.eu/scadplus/treaties/maastricht_en.htm
[3] europa.eu/scadplus/glossary/amsterdam_treaty_en.htm
[4] europa.eu/scadplus/glossary/nice_treaty_en.htm
[5] www.eu2007.de/en/News/Press_Releases/June/0623ER.html
[6] www.eurosceptic.com/
[7] europa.eu/abc/history/1970-1979/index_en.htm
[8] europa.eu/abc/history/1945-1959/index_en.htm
[9] www.unizar.es/euroconstitucion/Treaties/Treaty_Paris.htm
[10] europa.eu/50/index_en.htm
[11] europa.eu/scadplus/glossary/european_commission_en.htm
[12] ec.europa.eu/public_opinion/index_en.htm
[13] curia.europa.eu/en/instit/presentationfr/index_cje.htm
[14] en.euabc.com/word/280
[15] ec.europa.eu/civil_service/admin/index_en.htm
[16] www.euractiv.com/en/future-eu/eu-treaty-deal-meets-praise-criticism/article-164921
[17] www.brugesgroup.com/mediacentre/index.live?article=92
[18] www.palgrave.com/products/Catalogue.aspx?is=1403932395
[19] www.euractiv.com/en/future-eu/european-values-identity/article-154441
[20] www.ecb.eu/bc/intro/html/index.en.html#map
[21] www.ena.lu/mce.cfm

European Union: after the reform treaty

George Schöpflin
10 July 2007

> The new European accord achieves a workable compromise at the cost of avoiding the deeper issue of the union's democratic legitimacy, says George Schöpflin.

The "reform treaty" on which the European Union agreed in Brussels in the early hours of 23 June 2007 is both a compromise and an improvement on the two years of uncertainty that followed the French and Dutch rejections of the projected constitution in 2005. Nevertheless, the treaty raises a number of key issues that are likely to haunt the EU in the years to come, basically because as with many compromises, serious issues are unresolved.

At British and Dutch instigation, the reform treaty stipulates that the EU is to lose its symbols, such as the flag, the anthem and "Europe day." These losses may not appear significant at first sight, because symbolic elements tend to be dismissed as marginal. In reality they are a way to promote identification, in this case to strengthen the identification of the citizens of Europe with the EU, something that (notwithstanding Michael Bruter's argument in **openDemocracy**) is currently weak.

Not for nothing did the British and Dutch, the most Eurosceptic governments, focus on the symbols. If they were as irrelevant as people often think then their removal would not have been seen as important. But they were understood to be what they are—the underpinning of a state-like identity, of the EU as a political entity with its own autonomous political existence [1]. In a democratic world, this autonomous political field should have its own direct access to legitimation [2] by those affected by the EU's power—the citizens.

Intuitively or consciously, the anti-integrationist member-states recognised that the symbols [3] would enhance the relationship of the citizens of Europe with the EU—and saw this as weakening their own power over their citizens. Whether these relationships were really quite as zero-sum as this, these states did not want to take the risk of finding out whether establishing a stronger political relationship between the EU and the putative European demos would weaken the cohesiveness of the nation-state [4].

The nation: from danger to redoubt

The relationship between the EU and its member-states is and has always been an uneven one, in that integration can move forward only if the states agree on this. In effect, despite the EU possessing its own autonomous field of power [5], it lacks the capacity to enlarge this without the member-states's consent. The member-states will only do this if they think it is in their interest—the interest of the state as defined by the government of the day on an *ad-hoc* basis—or when there is pressure from below. This latter happens very rarely, if at all, not least because there are important forces in domestic politics determined to prevent a pro-EU mobilisation.

Also in **openDemocracy** on the European Union's Brussels summit:
John Palmer, "Europe: the square root of no" (20 June 2007)
Kalypso Nikolaïdis & Philippe Herzog, "Europe at fifty: a new single act" (21 June 2007)
John Palmer, "Europe's next steps" (26 June 2007)
Krzysztof Bobinski, "The Polish confusion" (28 June 2007)
Michael Bruter, "European Union: from backdoor to front" (3 July 2007)

The key here is a clear shift away from the assumption that the nation-state possessed of full sovereignty is a potential and, at times actual, danger for Europe. This was the default assumption for much of the post-war period [6], but that has changed. The problem, however, has not. This is the preventing of clashes that can and will arise from there being up to thirty-five high cultures living together in a confined geographic space with political power being structured around these cultural communities, i.e. nations. In the first half of the 20th century it generated disaster on disaster [7], but as memories have faded, so has the original impulse that gave rise to integration in Europe.

The original objective of European integration [8] was precisely to frame state sovereignty in a suprastate institution with explicit political goals, though using economic instruments to this end. From this perspective, the historic shift of the last fifteen-to-twenty years—the growing belief that too much was being settled in Europe that the state was better at—suggests that European integration has been a victim of its own success. The conflict-resolution mechanisms have been so successful as to make conflict unthinkable, hence unimaginable; from this it is a small step to say that they are superfluous. The change in generations has been a part of this story [9]; for those born after 1945, the second world war is simply too remote and irrelevant to today's concerns because Europe is doing quite well and other problems need more urgent attention.

This shift in attitudes has been accompanied by a dissatisfaction with the Europe that has actually been put in place, on the grounds that it is too remote and bureaucratic and too difficult to identify with. In reality, the symbolic "Brussels" so detested by the Eurosceptics is much smaller than widely believed—the EU commission has a staff of around 27,000, which is certainly smaller than the bureaucracy of a city the size of Liverpool. But—again—the "symbolics" do count and the impulse to identify with Europe has slackened both at the popular and the elite level. Thus a re-identification with the nation and, as a result, with the nation-state has returned imperceptibly, though obviously with varying intensity—in time and place, as well in form and content.

The sociological reality that European integration and political Europe [10] were always an elite activity has contributed to this disenchantment, given that at the popular level "Europe" always tended to be seen as an elite pastime, whereas the nation has retained its street-level resonance. That needs only an anti-European elite mobilisation to lift it into high political discourse. The member-state elites have frequently done this, by using the EU as the scapegoat for some particular unpopular move; London is particularly adept at doing this on a regular basis.

A treaty for tension

Another trigger of disillusion has been the unthinking insistence by an elite on a form of multiculturalism that was lived by the society in question as the downgrading of its own core values in the name of accommodating immigrants. The majority then became vulnerable to an anti-elite mobilisation which—when the elite launched a new phase of the European project—became a vote against Europe. In the Dutch case [11], this illustrates the complex interaction between different actors and different issues that at first sight have little to do with each other: European integration and immigrant integration (see Paul M. Sniderman & Louk Hagendoorn, *When Ways of Life Collide: Multiculturalism and Its Discontents in the Netherlands* [12] [Princeton University Press, 2007]). The majority saw its identity as bound up with sovereignty as a defence against the erosion of its core values and shifted against the perceived threat to that sovereignty, Europe.

Also in **openDemocracy** on the European Union in a decisive year:
Aurore Wanlin, "The European Union at fifty: a second life" (15 March 2007)
Krzysztof Bobinski, "European unity: reality and myth" (21 March 2007)
Frank Vibert, "The European Union in 2057" (22 March 2057)
Mats Engström, "Europe's green power" (26 March 2007)
Simon Berlaymont, "Tony Blair and Europe" (30 May 2007)

Thus anti-European sentiments have become a rallying-point for those hostile to an elite that is seen as favouring encroachments on one's sovereignty. This is quite correct, for this is exactly what integration is supposed to do—to dilute state sovereignty with the aim of producing security. But it is only dilution, not elimination. The tension between integration and state sovereignty will persist until such a time as the existing member-states definitively resolve the conflict between wanting more sovereignty or less. In this regard, the reformed treaty offers nothing that would help, but concentrates (as compromises are supposed to) on soluble problems instead.

The pivotal question, therefore, is whether a Europe of twenty-seven member-states can ever integrate further or whether the existing level of integration will be downgraded—or will the EU just stagnate? The almost certain answer is that the maximalists—those who want to go on with further integration—will conclude that the sovereignty-addicts are a nuisance they may as well be rid of, and that the goal of an all-European integration, "an ever-closer union" of the whole of Europe, may as well be abandoned. (It is worth noting here that one of the provisions of the constitution project [13] that has been retained is the exit clause. There is no exclusion clause, but Eurosceptics can now freely demand that their country leave [14] the EU and probably receive tacit sympathy from the maximalists. The United Kingdom and the Netherlands please note; Poland and the Czech Republic ditto).

The further implications of the treaty are that it moves Europe towards more inter-governmentalism and more functional integration at the same time. There is no doubt that this too will generate strains precisely because the two positions are pulling in opposite directions. Inter-governmentalism says that states may delegate and, presumably retrieve, powers granted to an agent of the states themselves. Functional activity, on the other hand, means that certain functions are more effectively exercised at the suprastate level, that certain powers are transferred to that level irreversibly, otherwise the agency will be subject to *ad hoc* political change (like a new government coming to office that does not see value in such power transfers).

These two forces, therefore, pull in opposite directions and can only be maintained in a kind of unstable equilibrium or perpetual fudge. At the very least, the demands of the inter-governmentalists will use up a great deal of time and energy to keep the equilibrium in being, while the maximalists will be tempted to go off and establish new, more tightly integrated [15] institutions of their own.

Democracy's pantomime-horse

Inter-governmentalism has a further, presumably intended consequence. It continues to keep the citizens of the EU [16] at arms length from its institutions and impedes their becoming a demos with political consciousness at the European level. As we have seen, the stripping away of the symbols was about this. But there is a deeper contradiction. Both the EU and its member-states are treaty-bound to support democracy and popular participation, but have very different ideas on what this actually implies [17].

For inter-governmentalists, identification, popular participation and legitimation should be structured around the member-state, leaving dealing with the EU to the elite and the government of the day. For the integrationists this involvement should be direct. Indeed, the logic of democracy supports this latter position—if it is accepted that the EU exists as an autonomous field of political power, then both popular participation and legitimation should be at that level.

In effect, what the inter-governmentalists say is that there is no such autonomous field, but equally they blame Brussels when it suits them, implying that there is. They claim that there is no European demos, only a series of member-state "demoi" and so should it stay, but at the same time operate as if the EU does function autonomously of them. This makes the inter-governmentalists free-riders on EU power. They have assented to it, but then deny that it exists. They silently welcome the democratic deficit and then blame the EU for being undemocratic. The member-state demos should not have much direct access to EU institutions, because that would erode state-level legitimacy. Equally a weak mediated relationship between the EU and a European demos [18] will pre-empt the possibility that the local demos might use EU provisions against the member-state. The charter of fundamental rights [19], from which the UK obtained an opt-out, is a good illustration.

Besides, the more the state-level demos gains knowledge of the EU, the more difficult it becomes for member-states to use the EU as a scapegoat for their own unpopular policies. This use of the EU is reminiscent of the communists in east-central Europe in the 1980s who were wont to say, "we would like to reform, but Moscow will not allow it." The inter-governmentalists have constructed an EU for their own purposes and want to keep it that way, because it suits them to have a weakly legitimated integration process that they can denounce as undemocratic.

A core Europe vs the rest?

The medium-to-long-term question which follows is: how long can the inter-governmentalists and integrationists remain together? What happens when the two clash? For the time being, the former can effectively slow down the integration process [20], though not bring it to a stop. The inclusion of climate change as a part of the EU's remit, something that was wholly absent when the draft constitution was negotiated, indicates that integration continues and is extending its scope. But if the wishes of the integrationists are continuously ignored, sooner or later they will begin seriously to contemplate a more highly integrated core Europe [21], obviously without the inter-governmentalists.

If European integration is the most effective conflict-resolution mechanism [22] ever devised—something that the inter-governmentalists do not recognise—then the tension between the two forces will have far-reaching consequences, not only for the inter-governmentalists, but also for the poorer member-states, which are most unlikely to be invited into this putative core Europe. Then the chances of conflict re-emerging cannot be ignored. The current friction between Poland and Germany is self-evidently eased by having both states inside the EU.

In the short term, the reform treaty will undoubtedly be a psychological boost—the European Union can operate again. But at the same time, there will now be greater caution about future projects on a Europe-wide scale. Maybe a project for twenty-seven states was always going to be too ambitious, but such considerations are not what the Europe of the ever-closer union is meant to be about.

URLS

[1] papers.ssrn.com/sol3/papers.cfm?abstract_id=513657
[2] www.palgrave-usa.com/catalog/product.aspx?isbn=1403921083
[3] europa.eu/50/anniversary_logo/index_en.htm
[4] www.akademika.no/vare.php?ean=9780415216296
[5] www.evropa.bg/en/del/europe-a-to-z/eu-institutions.html
[6] us.penguingroup.com/nf/Book/BookDisplay/0,,0_9781594200656,00.html
[7] www.randomhouse.ca/catalog/display.pperl?isbn=9780679757047
[8] www.eu-history.leidenuniv.nl/index.php3?m=1&c=3&garb=0.6256038390371258& session
[9] www.europeanstory.net/

[10] www.oup.com/uk/catalogue/?ci=9780199218677
[11] us.penguingroup.com/nf/Book/BookDisplay/0,,9781594201080,00.html
[12] press.princeton.edu/titles/8421.html
[13] www.euractiv.com/en/constitutional-treaty-key-elements/article-128513
[14] www.eurofaq.freeuk.com/
[15] www.dw-world.de/dw/article/0,2144,2636287,00.html
[16] www.palgrave.com/products/Catalogue.aspx?is=1403932395
[17] www.columbia.edu/cu/cup/catalog/data/023112/0231123760.HTM
[18] www.european-citizens-consultations.eu/3.0.html
[19] news.bbc.co.uk/1/hi/world/europe/6225580.stm
[20] europa.eu/50/index_en.htm
[21] www.eurointelligence.com/Article.620+M546c449b829.0.html
[22] www.historiasiglo20.org/europe/anteceden2.htm

Europe at fifty: towards a new single act

Kalypso Nicolaïdis, Philippe Herzog
21 June 2007

A fractious period in the European Union's internal politics could end if a new, modest but realistic strategic objective could be agreed, argue Philippe Herzog and Kalypso Nicolaidis.

The European Union may have turned fifty but it has yet to overcome its midlife crisis. At its summit in Brussels on 21-22 June 2007, the German presidency [1] has promised to do exactly that and fulfil the promise contained in its sober Berlin declaration, "to place the European Union on a renewed common basis before the European Parliament elections in 2009." There exist many divides in Europe; between rich and poor countries, old and new members, big and smaller states. But none has been more relevant to the German presidency than that between "constitutional purists" who argue that the eighteen states who have ratified the constitution cannot revisit their votes, and "constitutional minimalists" who point out that—according to rules of the games unanimously agreed to—the French and Dutch "no" votes cannot be overridden.

The combination of Angela Merkel's [2] determination to reach a compromise on the way forward and Nicolas Sarkozy's [3] determination to clear the ground for what most matters to him—his national programme of reform—has meant that we are heading towards a compromise at the Brussels summit around Sarkozy's idea of a "mini" or "simplified" treaty.

In this event, neither side will have won the day. Constitutional purists will have to give up the belief that with a bit of cosmetic surgery, like a "social annex," misguided publics can be made to vote the right way a second time. Even if they could, how sad and lacking in ambition it would be if the first constitution for Europe were to be passed with the narrowest of majorities, coercive popular "revotes" or discrete parliamentary decisions, against a background of both widespread opposition among European citizens and a general lack of enthusiasm. But minimalists too will need to accept that the constitutional ambition [4] will not simply disappear in the name of a Europe of results and pragmatism. Too much symbolic capital has been invested in it. In short, the idea of a constitution will and must remain (like Schrödinger's cat) both alive and dead in the years to come—even if under a different name [5] such as "constitutional charter."

Between maximum and minimum

This does not mean giving up on the idea. Opinion polls indicate that an overwhelming majority of Europeans think the European Union needs *a* constitution—not *this* constitution. If "making it our own" is to be the motto of their constituents, politicians must give time to time and resist the temptation to play Russian roulette with the idea of a constitution [6]. Indeed, pundits tend to forget the second part of Nicolas Sarkozy's message in autumn 2006 ("EU reform: what we need to do" [7]), which opened up such a perspective for after 2009. We believe even more time will be needed before Europeans are ready to engage in such an exercise, on this occasion in a truly inclusive and creative manner.

In short, the way forward lies with an old recipe of diplomatic and democratic deal-making [8]: sequencing—institutional reform in the short run followed by a "Europe of result" in the middle term, and a constitution in the longer term.

In the short term, the name of the game in Europe today is to produce institutional reform while avoiding referenda at all cost. For the constitutional purists this still means asking "what is the maximum we can get away with?;" for the minimalists, the question is "what is the minimum reform we must accept?"

In trying to cater to both these sides, the German fudge will set out the outline of a future text to be negotiated by an intergovernmental conference [9] in autumn 2007 which will recycle most of part one of the draft constitution "with the necessary presentational changes resulting from the return to the classical method of treaty change" as stated by the German presidency. In spite of such an apparently straightforward bargain, Merkel, Sarkozy and José Manuel Barroso [10] should not underestimate the conflictual dimension of this new treaty reform. The success of the whole enterprise depends on publics "buying in" the sleight of hand implied in relabelling tricks therein, including dropping the word "constitution."

The (semi-)consensual adoption of the institutional provisions of the constitutional treaty should not obscure the fact that very painful concessions were made at the time, not in the name of an "institutional package" but in the shadow of a perceived constitutional moment. If the small and medium countries ended up acquiescing in the death of the rotating presidency or the loss of their commissioner it was not because they "gained elsewhere in the package" but for fear of bringing down the constitutional dynamic [11] altogether. Why should they do so in the new context?

However contested [12] some of the issues surrounding the forthcoming intergovernmental conference, it will be even more necessary to achieve the ambitions of the policy-making phase that follows. The middle-term objective of this period, we believe, can be given both a name and antecedents: a new single act for a single Europe.

A restored momentum

The adoption of such a single act would depend on a dramatic surge of political acumen on the part of European leaders [13] and on their commitment to demonstrate that postponing in the long run the idea of a constitution or constitutional charter target is not synonymous with paralysis. After the 21-22 June summit [14] they would commit to launching a wide European debate on Europe's policies. In this context, the preparation of such a single act should be the main challenge for the 2009 elections of the European parliament.

Such an approach broadens the idea of a "mini-treaty" and anchors it where it should always have been: on a functionalist drive. The first single European act [15] masterminded by Jacques Delors that came into force in 1987 overcame what was called then Eurosclerosis by setting out a clear programme of action, with a method, a calendar and a deadline. Crucially, institutional reform, at the time a radical extension of qualified majority voting [16], was accepted by Margaret Thatcher, precisely because it was seen as a means to achieve a highly desirable end: the completion of the single market by 1992.

We can emulate this method today with a new single act whose goals are adapted to European reunification [17] in the post-cold-war era and to new challenges, such as globalisation and demography. In our view, such a single act should put forth a coherent and forward-looking programme of action in three core areas:

1. completing (yet again [18]) the single market that is after all Europe's proudest and longest-lasting achievement; this includes clarifying the status of public and private services

2. bringing together the disparate threads of the EU's core structuring policies—in climate change, energy security and pan-European infrastructures

3. delivering on Europe's role as a globally responsible actor, through a renewed statement of purpose and the development of practical instruments across relevant policy domains.

In a new single act, these programmes of action would be accompanied by a package of new institutional tools. The institutional treaty expected soon will probably be on a minimum package that would include a stable European council presidency, reform of the commission, and the installation of a foreign minister or representative along with a diplomatic service. The treaty will also, it is to be hoped, contain the consensual democracy-enhancing provisions of the draft constitutional treaty, extension of co-decision and qualified majority voting among them.

The single act would build within and around this framework to lay out a substantive agenda for the post-2009 parliament and commission.

Either way, institutional reform and policy agenda cannot be divorced and the single Act approach would link them. This would in turn pave the way—perhaps in a decade—to revisit the constitutional story. The approach we propose calls for modesty and realism. The new president of France has given up the idea of a renegotiation of the constitution in the short term followed by a new referendum. Britain and Poland [19] should also switch from veto politics to consensus-building. On this basis, the passing of a single act for a single Europe would recreate the momentum Europe now so dearly needs—as did its predecessor, before the upheavals which changed the face of Europe forever.

URLS

[1] www.eu2007.de/en/index.html
[2] www.bundesregierung.de/Webs/Breg/EN/Federal-Government/Chancellor/chancellor.html
[3] www.elysee.fr/elysee/elysee.fr/anglais/nicolas_sarkozy/biography/biography.78177.html
[4] www.unizar.es/euroconstitucion/Home.htm
[5] uk.reuters.com/article/worldNews/idUKL2087476020070620?src=062107_0724_TOPSTORY_eu_leaders_set_for_showdown
[6] en.euabc.com/word/2017
[7] www.europesworld.org/article.aspx?Id=2ada8047-7362-4d8e-85d1-62ad90b88da5
[8] www.bundesregierung.de/nn_6538/Content/EN/Artikel/2007/06/2007-06-20-europaeischer-rat-ankuendigung__en.html
[9] en.euabc.com/word/574
[10] ec.europa.eu/commission_barroso/president/index_en.htm
[11] www.euractiv.com/en/future-eu/eu-treaty-balance-leaders-flock-summit/article-164843
[12] www.ft.com/cms/s/7c29c26c-1e48-11dc-bc22-000b5df10621,dwp_uuid=70662e7c-3027-11da-ba9f-00000e2511c8.html
[13] www.euractiv.com/en/opinion/merkel-barroso-best-lead-eu-poll/article-164721
[14] www.consilium.europa.eu/showPage.asp?id=668&lang=en
[15] www.historiasiglo20.org/europe/acta.htm
[16] en.euabc.com/word/783
[17] europa.eu/50/index_en.htm
[18] www.europesworld.org/EWSettings/Article/tabid/78/Default.aspx?Id=8b62a193-08c7-496e-b090-f377494b310c
[19] www.euractiv.com/en/future-eu/barroso-warns-poland-uk-risks-blocking-eu-treaty/article-164750

Resources: a brief guide to suggested books, websites, institutes and think-tanks for further research, reading, study and engagement about the European Union and Europe as a whole

Books

Michael Bruter Citizens of Europe? The Emergence of a Mass European Identity (Palgrave Macmillan, 2005)
www.palgrave.com/products/title.aspx?is=1403932395

Barbara Einhorn Citizenship in a Uniting Europe (Palgrave, 2006)
www.palgrave.com/politics/eu/index.asp

Financial Times Business / Agora Projects European Union: The next 50 Years (2007)
eubookshop.com/1/187

Edgar Grande & Ulrich Beck Cosmopolitan Europe (Polity, 2007)
www.polity.co.uk/book.asp?ref=9780745635620

Stanislav J Kirschbaum Central European History and the European Union (Palgrave, 2007)
www.palgrave.com/products/title.aspx?PID=280310

Janet Mather Legitimating the European Union: Aspirations, Inputs and Performances (Palgrave Macmillan, 2006)
www.palgrave-usa.com/catalog/product.aspx?isbn=1403921083

Sophie Meunier & Kathleen R McNamara, eds. Making History: European Integration and Institutional Change at Fifty (Oxford University Press, 2007)
www.oup.com/uk/catalogue/?ci=9780199218677

Tony Judt Postwar: A History of Europe since 1945 (Penguin, 2005)
us.penguingroup.com/nf/Book/BookDisplay/0,,9780143037750,
00.html?breadcrumbList=judt&bcPath=c590611%2D00000000%23%
23%2D1%23%23%2D1%7E%7Eq6a756474&searchProfile=US-590611-
global&strSrchSql=judt

John Pinder & Simon Usherwood The European Union: A Very Short Introduction (Oxford University Press, forthcoming 2008) www.us.oup.com/us/catalog/general/subject/Politics/ComparativePolitics/EuropeanUnion/?view=usa&ci=9780199233977

Frank Vibert Europe Simple, Europe Strong: The Future of European Governance (Polity, 2001) www.polity.co.uk/book.asp?ref=9780745628530

Institutes and think-tanks

Centre for Liberal Strategies
www.cls-sofia.org/cgi-bin/public/index.cgi

Centre for European Policy Studies www.ceps.be/index3.php

Centre for European Reform www.cer.org.uk/

Centre for the New Europe www.cne.org/

Confrontations Europe
www.confrontations.org/spip.php?rubrique46

European Council on Foreign Relations
www.onevoiceforeurope.eu/

European Institute, London School of Economics
www.lse.ac.uk/collections/europeanInstitute/

European Policy Forum www.epfltd.org/index.htm

European Policy Centre www.epc.eu/

European Union Program, Princeton University
http://www.princeton.edu/ europe/index.htm

Foreign Policy Centre fpc.org.uk/

Unia & Polska Foundation www.eureferenda.org/

Websites—official, research, advocacy, media

Café Babel www.cafebabel.com/en/default.asp

Council of Europe www.coe.int/

EUObserver euobserver.com/
EurActiv www.euractiv.com/en/
Europa: European Union gateway europa.eu/index_en.htm
Europa: European Union glossary
  europa.eu/scadplus/glossary/index_en.htm
Europa: The history of the European Union
  europa.eu/abc/history/index_en.htm
Europa: 50th Anniversary of the treaty of Rome
  europa.eu/50/index_en.htm
Europe 2020 www.europe2020.org/?lang=en
European Center for Minority Issues www.ecmi.de
European Citizens' Initiative
  www.democracy-international.org/eci.html
European Council on Refugees and Exiles www.ecre.org
European Story www.europeanstory.net/
European Union Agency for Fundamental Rights
  fra.europa.eu/fra/index.php
European Union database
  www.eurunion.org/infores/besteuwebsites.htm
European Union on the web
  www.palgrave.com/politics/eu/euontheweb.asp
EuropeVoice www.europeanvoice.com/
Eurozine www.eurozine.com/
HistoriasigloXX: The History of European Union and European Citizenship
  www.historiasiglo20.org/europe/cronologia.htm
International Helsinki Federation for Human Rights
  www.ihf-hr.org
Leiden University: History of European Integration
  www.eu-history.leidenuniv.nl/index.php3?m=7&c=13&garb=0.
  25204500638639276&session=
Newropeans Magazine www.newropeans-magazine.org/index.php
The European Constitution—Documents
  www.unizar.es/euroconstitucion/Home.htm

# Authors of the articles

Ash Amin

Ash Amin is professor [1] of geography at Durham University. His research and publications have dealt with regional development and socio-economic inequality in Europe, the social economy of the city, and the socio-political evolution of multicultural and multi-ethnic societies within the European Union.
Among his books is (as co-author) *Architectures of Knowledge: Firms, Capabilities and Communities* (Oxford University Press, 2004)
Article in this book [p. 150].
A full list of Ash Amin's articles on **openDemocracy** is here:
www.opendemocracy.net/author/Ash_Amin.jsp

Katinka Barysch

Katinka Barysch is chief economist [2]. at the Centre for European Reform. The article is largely based on the proceedings of the third Bosphorus Conference 2006 [3], organised by the British Council, Tesev and the CER in Istanbul on 15-16 September 2006.
Article in this book [p. 125].
A full list of Katinka Barysch's articles on **openDemocracy** is here:
www.opendemocracy.net/author/Katinka_Barysch.jsp

Simon Berlaymont

Simon Berlaymont is a pseudonym. The writer has extensive professional knowledge of the inner workings of the European Union.
Articles in this book [pp. 81, 139].
A full list of Simon Berlaymont's articles on **openDemocracy** is here:
www.opendemocracy.net/author/Simon_Berlaymont.jsp

Krzysztof Bobinski

Krzysztof Bobinski works at the Unia & Polska Foundation [4]—a pro-European NGO in Warsaw. He was the *Financial Times*'s correspondent in Warsaw.
Articles in this book [pp. 76, 101].

A full list of Krzysztof Bobinski's articles on **openDemocracy** is here:
www.opendemocracy.net/author/Krzysztof_Bobinski.jsp

Michael Bruter

Michael Bruter is senior lecturer in European politics at the London School of Economics and Political Science. He is the author of *Citizens of Europe? The Emergence of a Mass European Identity* [5] (Palgrave Macmillan, 2005). His homepage is here: www.michaelbruter.org/
A full list of Michael Bruter's articles on **openDemocracy** is here:
www.opendemocracy.net/user/502899

Ian Christie

Ian Christie is a writer, researcher and local government policymaker, based in London. He is joint head of environmental and economic policy at Surrey County Council in southeast England. He is an associate of the Green alliance and of the New Economics Foundation. He is a visiting professor of sustainable development at Surrey University and has advised many public agencies and businesses in the UK on environmental policy, sustainability and analysis of political and social change. His publications include *From Here to Sustainability: politics in the real world* (Earthscan, 2001, with Diane Warburton).
Article in this book [p. 29].
A full list of Ian Christie's articles on **openDemocracy** is here:
www.opendemocracy.net/author/Ian_Christie.jsp

Mats Engström

Mats Engström is editorial writer at the Swedish newspaper *Aftonbladet*. He was special advisor and deputy state secretary to Anna Lindh from 1994-2001. He is author of *Rebooting Europe: Digital Deliberation and European Democracy* (Foreign Policy Centre, 2002 [6]). His homepage is here: www.matsengstrom.se
Article in this book [p. 69].
A full list of Mats Engström's articles on **openDemocracy** is here:
www.opendemocracy.net/author/Mats_Engstrom.jsp

Authors of the articles

David Hayes

David Hayes is deputy editor of **openDemocracy**. He has written textbooks on human rights and terrorism, and was a contributor to *Town and Country* (Jonathan Cape, 1998). His work has been published in *PN Review*, the *Irish Times*, the *New Statesman* and *The Absolute Game*.
Introduction to this book [p. 11].
A full list of David Hayes's articles on **openDemocracy** is here:
www.opendemocracy.net/author/David_Hayes.jsp

Judith Herrin

Judith Herrin is Professor of Late Antique and Byzantine Studies at King's College, London, and Director of the Centre for Hellenic Studies. Her books include *The Formation of Christendom* (Princeton University Press, 1987), *A Medieval Miscellany* (Penguin, 2000) and *Woman in Purple: Rulers of Medieval Byzantium* (Princeton University Press, 2000). In 2002 she was awarded the Golden Cross of Honour by the president of the Hellenic Republic of Greece.
Article in this book [p. 13].
A full list of Judidh Herrin's articles on **openDemocracy** is here:
www.opendemocracy.net/author/Judith_Herrin.jsp

Philippe Herzog

Philippe Herzog is director of the think-tank Confrontations-Europe [7]. His homepage is here: www.confrontations.org/philippeherzog/biographie/index.php
Article in this book [p. 193].
A full list of Philippe Herzog's articles on **openDemocracy** is here:
www.opendemocracy.net/user/502441

Reinhard Hesse

Reinhard Hesse (1956-2004) was a writer, journalist and foreign correspondent for several German newspapers and magazines. He advised and wrote speeches for Germany's Chancellor, Gerhard Schröder. Among his books is *Ground Zero: Der Westen und die islamische Welt gegen den globalen Djihad* (Econ Verlag, 2002 [8]). He died [9] in October 2004.
Articles in this book [pp. 21, 50].

A full list of Reinhard Hesse's articles on **openDemocracy** is here:
www.opendemocracy.net/author/Reinhard_Hesse.jsp

Paul Hilder

Paul Hilder is a co-founder of **openDemocracy**, and an independent adviser and writer working on democratic renewal, Europe, and the middle east. He is middle-east campaign director of Avaaz.org, a fellow of The Young Foundation [www.icstudies.ac.uk], and senior policy consultant to the Middle East Policy Initiative Forum. His books include (as co-editor) *Peace Fire: Fragments from the Israel-Palestine Story* (2002) and (as editor) *The Democratic Papers* (2004 [10]). He blogs at gathering.typepad.com
Article in this book [p. 35].
A full list of Paul Hilder's articles on **openDemocracy** is here:
www.opendemocracy.net/author/Paul_Hilder.jsp

Kirsty Hughes

Kirsty Hughes is a researcher and commentator on European affairs. She was formerly senior research fellow at the Centre for European Policy Studies [11] (CEPS) in Brussels, and coordinator for the European Policy Institutes Network [12] (EPIN).
Article in this book [p. 89].
A full list of Kirsty Hughes's articles on **openDemocracy** is here:
www.opendemocracy.net/author/Kirsty_Hughes.jsp

Ivan Krastev

Ivan Krastev is chair of the Centre for Liberal Strategies [13] in Sofia, Bulgaria. He served as the executive director [14] of the International Commission on the Balkans.
Article in this book [p. 132].
A full list of Ivan Krastev's articles on **openDemocracy** is here:
www.opendemocracy.net/author/Ivan_Krastev.jsp

Petr Mach

Petr Mach is an economist, researcher and advisor, working in the Czech Republic. He has published the newsletter *Laisser Faire* since 1998, and worked at the Centre for Economics and Politics in Prague since 1999. His

Authors of the articles

homepage is here: www.petrmach.cz/cze/stranka.php?sekce=12
Article in this book [p. 57].
A full list of Petr Mach's articles on **openDemocracy** is here:
www.opendemocracy.net/author/Petr_Mach.jsp

Kalypso Nicolaïdis

Kalypso Nicolaïdis is lecturer in international relations at Oxford University, chair of south European studies at Oxford, and professorial chair on visions of Europe at the College of Europe, Bruges. She has published widely on constitutional politics in the European Union, enlargement, comparative federalism and issues of legitimacy, global governance, and negotiation theory. Her works include *The Federal Vision: Legitimacy and Levels of Governance in the US and the EU* (Oxford University Press, 2001 [15]) and *We the peoples of Europe* (Foreign Affairs, 2004 [16]). Her homepage is here:
www.sant.ox.ac.uk/esc/knicolaidis/
Articles in this book [pp. 159, 193].
A full list of Kalypso Nicolaïdis's articles on **openDemocracy** is here:
www.opendemocracy.net/author/Kalypso_Nicolaidis.jsp

John Palmer

John Palmer has written about European affairs for many years, notably as European editor of the *Guardian*. He is former political director of the European Policy Centre [17] and is now a member of its governing board.
Article in this book [p. 163].
A full list of John Palmer's articles on **openDemocracy** is here:
www.opendemocracy.net/author/John_Palmer.jsp

Jeremy Rifkin

Jeremy Rifkin is president of the Foundation on Economic Trends [18] in Washington, D.C. His seventeen books include *The European Dream: How Europe's Vision of the Future is Quietly Eclipsing the American Dream* (Tarcher/Penguin, 2004).
Article in this book [p. 57].
A full list of Jeremy Rifkin's articles on **openDemocracy** is here:
www.opendemocracy.net/author/Jeremy_Rifkin.jsp

Pierre Rosanvallon

Pierre Rosanvallon is a professor at the Collège de France and L'Ecole de Hautes Etudes en Science Sociales (EHESS [19]), Paris. The most recent of his many books is *The Demands of Liberty: Civil Society Society in France since the Revolution* (Harvard University Press, 2007)
Article in this book [p. 64].
A full list of Pierre Rosanvallon's articles on **openDemocracy** is here:
www.opendemocracy.net/author/Pierre_Rosanvallon.jsp

George Schöpflin

George Schöpflin is a member of the European parliament for Fidesz (Hungarian Civic Union) and was Jean Monnet professor [20] of politics at University College London.
Article in this book [p. 185].
A full list of George Schöpflin's articles on **openDemocracy** is here:
www.opendemocracy.net/author/George_Schopflin.jsp

Ilija Trojanow

Ilija Trojanow is an award-winning writer [21]. He was born in Bulgaria in 1965, found political asylum in Germany after fleeing the country, and lives in Cape Town. Among his many books is *Along the Ganges* [22] (Haus Publishing, 2005).
Article in this book [p. 120].
A full list of Ilija Trojanow's articles on **openDemocracy** is here:
www.opendemocracy.net/author/Ilija_Trojanow.jsp

Theo Veenkamp

Theo Veenkamp was head of the Netherlands Agency for the Reception of Asylum-Seekers and head of strategy at the Dutch ministry of justice. He is now active as an essayist and adviser. He was first co-author of *People Flow: managing migration in a new European commonwealth*, Demos/**openDemocracy** (2003 [23])
Article in this book [p. 94].
A full list of Theo Veenkamp's articles on **openDemocracy** is here:
www.opendemocracy.net/author/Theo_Veenkamp.jsp

Authors of the articles

Frank Vibert

Frank Vibert is director of the European Policy Forum [24]. He is the author of *Europe Simple, Europe Strong: The Future of European Governance* (Polity, 2001 [25]) and *The Rise of the Unelected: Democracy and the New Separation of Powers* (Cambridge University Press, 2007 [26]).
Articles in this book [pp. 108, 173].
A full list of Frank Vibert's articles on **openDemocracy** is here:
www.opendemocracy.net/author/Frank_Vibert.jsp

Aurore Wanlin

Aurore Wanlin works for Publicis Consultants in Paris. She was formerly a research fellow at the Centre for European Reform in London.
Articles in this book [pp. 115, 167].
A full list of Aurore Wanlin's articles on **openDemocracy** is here:
www.opendemocracy.net/author/Aurore_Wanlin.jsp

URLS

[1] www.geography.dur.ac.uk/information/staff/amin.html
[2] www.cer.org.uk/about_new/about_cerpersonnel_barysch.html
[3] www.britishcouncil.org.tr/BOSPHORUS/default.asp?c=12&s=
[4] www.eureferenda.org/
[5] www.palgrave.com/products/Catalogue.aspx?is=1403932395
[6] fpc.org.uk/publications/61
[7] www.confrontations.org/spip.php?rubrique46
[8] www.perlentaucher.de/buch/10561.html
[9] www.timesonline.co.uk/article/0,,60-1374830,00.html
[10] users.ox.ac.uk/~ssfc0041/democraticpapers.pdf
[11] www.ceps.be/index.php
[12] www.epin.org/
[13] www.cls-sofia.org/about_us/index-en.htm
[14] www.balkan-commission.org/
[15] www.us.oup.com/us/catalog/general/subject/?view=usa&sf=toc&ci=0199245002
[16] www.foreignaffairs.org/20041101faessay83609/kalypso-nicolaidis/we-the-peoples-of-europe.html
[17] www.theepc.be/
[18] www.foet.org
[19] www.ehess.fr/html/html/7.html
[20] www.sciforum.hu/index.php?image=speakers&content=sp_schopflin
[21] www.nthposition.com/author.php?authid=177
[22] www.life-and-times.co.uk/travel/index.shtml
[23] www.demos.co.uk/catalogue/peopleflow_page247.aspx
[24] www.epfltd.org/msg10.htm
[25] www.polity.co.uk/book.asp?ref=0745628532
[26] www.cambridge.org/uk/catalogue/catalogue.asp?isbn=0521694140

www.ingramcontent.com/pod-product-compliance
Ingram Content Group UK Ltd.
Pitfield, Milton Keynes, MK11 3LW, UK
UKHW041438180426
11947UKWH00007B/510